MANIFESTING YOUR DPS ~ DREAM POSITIONING SYSTEM

YOUR BLUEPRINT TOWARDS SUCCESS

DAVID B. RICH

DEDICATION

To my dearest mother, Veronica A. Rich,

This book, "Manifesting your DPS (Dream Positioning System)," is dedicated to you, my incredible and inspiringmother. You were not just a guiding light in my life, but also a beacon of strength and resilience. You taught me how to embrace life, no matter the challenges or situations we face.

Your unwavering support and belief in me have been the fuel for my dreams. You were always my biggest fan, cheering me on and encouraging me to pursue my endeavors with passion and dedication. Your spirit and infectious smile brought light to the world, touching the hearts of everyone you met.

I remember how "I Hope you Dance" by Lee Ann Womackwas your favorite song, and it perfectly encapsulated youroutlook on life. You believed that when life presents us with a choice to sit it out or dance, we should always choose to dance! That affirmation has stayed with me, reminding me to embrace every opportunity and live life to the fullest.

Even after you transitioned to the spiritual realm, our conversation resonated deeply within me. Your simple yet profound words, "Be Great!" continue to echo in my heart. They serve as a constant reminder that greatness lies within me and that I must strive to achieve it in all aspects of my life.

It is with immense love, gratitude, and admiration that I dedicate this book to you, my beloved mother. As I embark on this journey of empowering others to manifesttheir dreams and find their true purpose, I carry your teachings, love, and indomitable spirit with me. You will forever be my guiding star, my inspiration, and my greatest source of strength.

With all my love, ***Your***

son

David B. Rich

PREFACE

Embarking on this journey with you is an honor and a privilege, as we dive deep into the transformative concept of the Dream Positioning System (DPS). DPS is more than just a set of strategies; it's your comprehensive blueprint for success, designed to help you bridge the gap betweenyour aspirations and the reality you desire.

My own quest for understanding the principles that lead to personal growth and accomplishment has been heavilyinfluenced by two remarkable individuals: Daisaku Ikeda and Les Brown.

Daisaku Ikeda, a global leader and advocate for peace and happiness, has been a guiding light for me and countless others. His philosophy of establishing global peace and eternal happiness one heart at a time has been a profound inspiration. Ikeda's teachings emphasize the transformative power of faith, determination, and action in achieving our goals and dreams. His wisdom has been instrumental in my journey towards understanding the significance of visualization, belief, and the relentless pursuit of one's purpose.

Les Brown, a renowned motivational speaker, entered my life during a business conference I attended. His powerful words ignited a spark within me, revealing my calling as amotivational speaker. Learning from him and becoming a member of Les Brown's speaking team taught me the art of speaking from the heart to touch the hearts of others. It's through Les Brown's mentorship that I mastered the skill of inspiring others through the lens of my life's journey.

There's a saying that goes, "There are two great days in a person's life—the day they were born and the day they discover why." For me, meeting Les Brown was that pivotal moment when I discovered my "why" andembarked on a mission to inspire and empower others.

As we journey through the DPS together, we'll explore theinner workings of this transformative system. We'll dive into the principles of visualization, belief, unlocking your inner potential, setting clear and inspiring goals, overcoming limiting beliefs, cultivating a success mindset, taking inspired action, and persisting through challenges. Each chapter will be enriched with real-life stories, inspiring quotes, and practical strategies to help you manifest your dreams and live a life of purpose and contribution.

The path ahead promises transformation, empowerment,and the unwavering belief that you have the power to choose your priorities and shape your destiny. Your dreams are not distant fantasies but potential realities waiting to be awakened. As we embark on this journey together, may you find inspiration and guidance within these pages, igniting the fire of your dreams and positioning yourself for a life of fulfillment and purpose.

GPS (Global Positioning System):

GPS, or Global Positioning System, is a navigation system that allows individuals to determine their precise location on Earth's surface. It consists of a network of satellites, ground control stations, and GPS receivers. The primary principle behind GPS is the triangulation of signals from these satellites to calculate a user's exact position.

Triangulation of Signals:

GPS relies on the concept of triangulation, where signals are transmitted from multiplesatellites in space to a GPS receiver on the ground. Each satellite emits a signal containing information about its position and the precise time the signal was sent. When the GPS receiver receives these signals, it uses the time delay between when the signal was transmitted and when it was received to calculate the distance from each satellite.

Calculation of Position:

By measuring the distance from atleast four satellites, the GPS receiver can determine its latitude, longitude, altitude, and speed. This information is then used to provide accurate navigation and location data to the user.

Widespread Use:

GPS technology is widely used for various purposes, including vehicle navigation, tracking, mapping, surveying, and more. It has become an essentialtool in everyday life, guiding individuals and vehicles to their destinations with precision.

Your Dream Positioning System (DPS) is a metaphorical system designed to help you navigate and achieve your life's goals and dreams. While it doesn't have a physical presence like a GPS (Global Positioning System), it serves a similar purpose in guiding you toward your desire destination in life.

Here's an overview of what your DPS entails:

- **Setting Clear Goals and Dreams:** Your DPS begins withsetting clear and specific goals and dreams for yourself. These could be related to your career, personal life, relationships, health, or any other area that is important to you. Your goals and dreams provide the coordinates foryour life's journey.

- **Visualization:** Visualization is a powerful tool in your DPS. It involves mentally seeing yourself already in possession of your goals and dreams. This helps you create a vivid mental image of your desired destination, making it more tangible and achievable.

- **Planning:** Just as a GPS provides you with a route to follow, your DPS involves creating a plan to reach your goals. This plan includes actionable steps, timelines, and milestones to track your progress along the way.

- **Belief and Mindset:** Believing in yourself and your ability to achieve your dreams is a fundamental aspect of your DPS. A positive and determined mindset is like the fuel that propels you forward on your journey.

- **Acting:** Your DPS encourages you to take consistent and purposeful action toward your goals. It's not enough to dream and plan; you must actively work toward your aspirations.

- **Adaptability:** Just as a GPS may reroute you due to unexpected roadblocks, your DPS allows for course corrections. You should be willing to adapt and make changes to your plan as needed to overcome challenges and obstacles.

- **Learning and Growth:** Your DPS acknowledges that the journey toward your dreams is also a path of personal growth and development. Embracing new knowledge and experiences along the way enriches your life.

- **Empowerment:** Like a GPS empowers you with the knowledge of where you are and where you're going, your DPS empowers you to take control of your life and create the future you desire.

- **Persistence and Resilience:** Your DPS recognizes that challenges and setbacks are part of any journey. It encourages you to persist and be resilient in the face of difficulties, knowing that they are steppingstones to your ultimate destination.

- **Fulfillment:** Ultimately, your DPS is designed to lead you to a place of fulfillment and achievement. It helps you align your actions with your deepest desires, creating a sense of purpose and contentment.

Comparing GPS to DPS (Dream Positioning System): Now, let's compare GPS to your DPS (Dream Positioning System), which is a metaphorical system for navigating life's goals and dreams:

- **Principle of Guidance:** GPS provides guidance for physical navigation by triangulating signals from satellites, whereas DPS offers guidance for personal and goal- oriented navigation. Both systems offer a means of direction, whether in the physical world or within one's life.

- **Setting Clear Intentions:** In GPS, the receiver needs to have a clear intention of determining its position and destination. Similarly, in DPS, individuals set clear intentions by visualizing and defining their goals and dreams.

- **Belief and Trust:** Users of GPS trust that the system will provide accurate information. In DPS, belief and trust are crucial in believing that your goals are attainable and that your actions will lead to success.

- **Action and Progress:** GPS helps users act by providing real-time information on their location and route. DPS encourages individuals to act aligned with their goals, using visualization, planning, and action steps.

- **Empowerment:** Both GPS and DPS empower individuals. GPS empowers users to reach their physical destinations efficiently, while DPS empowers individuals to manifest their dreams and achieve their life's purpose.

A GPS can detect traffic delays and even road closures. Your DPS also can navigate you through challenges and difficulties.

A GPS may sometimes reroute you due to poor travel conditions, and by implementing the tools and strategies of my DPS, you may find that rerouting yourself and your mindset will guide you to your dreams. As a pilot chart outits intended route, once in the air, they will always make course corrections due to weather or any number of turbulent and time-draining conditions. However, never loses sight of its destination.

While your DPS doesn't operate like a physical GPS, it serves as a mental and emotional guide for navigating thejourney of your life. It helps you stay focused on your goals, make informed decisions, and stay on course even when faced with detours.

One is for physical navigation and the other for life'snavigation—they share common principles of guidance, setting clear intentions, belief, acting, and empowerment.A GPS leads individuals to specific physical destinations, while DPS guides them toward realizing their dreams andaspirations. Both systems emphasize the importance of direction, trust, and taking steps to reach a desired outcome. However, Your DPS is a powerful tool for personal growth, empowerment, and the realization of your dreams.

CHAPTER LIST

BOOK INTRODUCTION

In a world filled with opportunities and endless potential, have you ever wondered why some people seem to effortlessly manifest their dreams while others struggle to make progress? Welcome to "Manifest Your Dreams with DPS: A Path to Abundance and Fulfillment." This book unveils the transformative power of the Dream Positioning System (DPS), a proven methodology that will guide you towards manifesting your deepest desires and aspirations.

Drawing inspiration from the timeless wisdom of Napoleon Hill's "Think and Grow Rich," the insightful writings of Daisaku Ikeda, the motivational teachings of Les Brown, the leadership principles of John Maxwell, the financial wisdom of Robert Kiyosaki, and the mindfulness lessons of Jay Shetty's "Think like a Monk," this book provides a comprehensive blueprint for achieving your dreams.

CHAPTER 1

INTRODUCTION TO
DREAM POSITIONING SYSTEM (DPS)

"If you know where you're going ~ It doesn't matter where you are at!"

- David B. Rich

In a world driven by dreams and aspirations, where each of us harbors the desire to achieve greatness, it's not uncommon to find ourselves at crossroads, questioning our purpose and the path to our deepest desires. Many ofus have read books, attended seminars, and even receivedguidance from mentors. All in the pursuit of realizing our dreams. Yet, for some reason, success often feels elusive.It's as though we're standing on the shore, gazing at the distant island of our dreams, but the bridge to reach it remains hidden. If you've ever found yourself in this predicament, wondering why your dreams remain just beyond your grasp, then you've come to the right place. The journey to manifesting your dreams begins here, withthe introduction to the Dream Positioning System (DPS), atransformative methodology that holds the key to unlocking your full potential and turning your dreams intoreality.

Before we dive into the intricacies of DPS, let's take a moment to ponder the unseen forces that shape our lives.Every day, we are bombarded with thoughts, emotions, and external influences that affect our decisions, actions, and ultimately, our destinies. These forces can either propel us toward our dreams or hold us back in the quagmire of mediocrity. Consider for a moment the powerof your thoughts. Thoughts are not mere fleeting mental occurrences; they are the architects of your reality. Each thought you entertain carries with it the potential to shape your future. Your beliefs, whether empowering or limiting, act as filters through which you perceive the world and determine what is possible for you.

Now, add to this the influence of the people around you—the friends, family, colleagues, and mentors who shape your mindset, offer guidance, or inadvertently plant seeds of doubt. Their impact on your life journey cannot be overstated. Furthermore, the environment you inhabit— the culture, values, and opportunities it presents—plays a significant role in shaping your aspirations and the strategies you employ to achieve them. These external factors create the backdrop against which your dreams unfold.

The desire to manifest one's dreams is universal. It transcends geographical boundaries, cultural differences, and socioeconomic status. Whether you're a young entrepreneur yearning to build a thriving business empire, a student aiming for academic excellence, a parent aspiring to provide a secure future for your children, or an artist with a vision to inspire the world—your dreams are the compass that guides your life. So, what sets apart those who manifest their dreams from those who merely dream them? The answer lies in the systematic approach they take and the tools they employ to navigate the complex terrain of life.

The Birth of Dream Positioning System (DPS)

The Dream Positioning System (DPS) was born out of my relentless quest to uncover the formula for turning dreams into reality. It's the culmination of wisdom drawn from ancient philosophy, modern psychology, success principles, and the experiences of countless individuals who have walked the path of achievement.

To understand DPS, we must first dissect its components:

Dreams: At the heart of DPS lies your dreams—the visions, goals, and aspirations that stir your soul. These dreams are not mere fantasies; they are the blueprints of your destiny. They represent what you truly desire in life, whether it's financial abundance, a fulfilling career, harmonious relationships, vibrant health, or spiritual enlightenment. These are not vague wishes but clear, vibrant visions of what you want to achieve in life. Dreams serve as your North Star, guiding you through the twists and turns of your journey.

Positioning: the term "positioning" refers to the deliberate act of placing yourself in a strategic stance to align with your dreams. It involves identifying your unique strengths, talents, and capabilities and positioning them in a way that maximizes their impact. It also means creating an environment conducive to the realization of your dreams.

It involves the strategic positioning of your resources, talents, and efforts to align with your dreams. It's about creating the conditions for success, much like a gardener tending to the soil to nurture the growth of a prized flower.

System: DPS is not a random collection of ideas but a structured system—a step-by-step guide that takes you from where you are now to where you want to be. It provides you with the tools, techniques, and principles necessary to navigate the challenges and uncertainties of your journey. It is a systematic approach to manifesting your dreams. It provides a structured framework, and a process to follow. It's not about wishful thinking; it's about intentional, purposeful action.

In essence, DPS is the roadmap to your dreams. It's the compass that helps you navigate the vast sea of possibilities and chart a course towards your desired destination. It's the bridge between where you are today and where you envision yourself in the future.

You might be wondering why DPS is significant in the grand scheme of manifesting your dreams. To answer thatquestion, let's consider the alternative—a life without a clear and systematic approach to your dreams.

Without a roadmap like DPS, you may find yourself wandering aimlessly through life, reacting to external circumstances rather than proactively shaping your destiny. You may experience moments of inspiration and motivation, but these fleeting sparks are often doused bythe daily grind, self-doubt, and distractions.

DPS empowers you to take control of your life's narrative. It offers a structured approach that not only keeps you focused on your dreams but also equips you with the toolsto overcome obstacles and challenges along the way. It's a framework for consistent progress, guiding you throughthe storms and uncertainties of life with unwavering clarity.

In the chapters to come, we will delve deeper into each component of DPS, exploring how to identify your dreams,position yourself strategically, and implement a systematic approach to manifesting your deepest desires.We will draw inspiration from the wisdom of visionaries like Napoleon Hill, Daisaku Ikeda, Les Brown, JohnMaxwell, Robert Kiyosaki, and many other leaders and scholars for whom I have had the privilege to have studied under. Weaving their insights into the fabric of DPS to create a comprehensive guide for your journey.

But first, take a moment to reflect on your dreams. What is it that you truly desire? What does your ideal future looklike? As we embark on this transformative journey together, remember that the first step towardsmanifesting your dreams is to envision them clearly. DPS is here to help you turn those visions into reality, one stepat a time.

In a world where dreams are the currency of hope and ambition, where every individual harbors aspirations thatflicker like stars in the night sky, there exists a common yearning—to turn those dreams into reality. This chapter marks the beginning of a journey, a journey that will takeyou from the realm of mere desires to the realm of tangible achievements. Welcome to the world of the Dream Positioning System, or DPS.

Dreams are the tapestry upon which the human experience is woven. From the moment we take our first breath, we begin to dream. As children, we dream of becoming astronauts, explorers, superheroes, and princesses. As we grow, our dreams evolve— perhaps intothe pursuit of a fulfilling career, a loving family, financial security, or a legacy that transcends time.

These dreams aren't just idle fantasies; they are the heartbeat of our existence. They infuse our lives with purpose, providing direction and motivation. Dreams havethe power to inspire us to reach higher, to become more than we ever thought possible. They are the stars that guide us through life's vast expanse.

Yet, for all their power and beauty, dreams are delicate. They can be easily obscured by the storms of doubt, drowned out by the cacophony of societal expectations, and buried beneath the weight of our own insecurities. The call of our dreams persists, but the path to realizing them can seem elusive.

The pursuit of dreams has led countless individuals on a quest for answers. How do we navigate the labyrinth of life to reach the treasure chest of our dreams? Can we finda blueprint, a guide that illuminates the path, a system that transforms dreams into reality?

This is where the Dream Positioning System, or DPS, enters the picture. DPS is not just a method; it's a philosophy, a mindset, and a way of life. It is the bridge that connects the realm of dreams to the realm of manifestation.

You might wonder why DPS is essential in your quest to manifest your dreams. After all, can't you simply work hard, stay focused, and hope for the best? Whiledetermination and focus are crucial, DPS serves as a guiding light in the darkness.

Without a system like DPS, you may find yourself wandering in circles, expending energy without a clear direction. Dreams may remain abstract concepts rather than tangible goals. Doubt and uncertainty may cast shadows over your journey, making it difficult to stay the course.

DPS provides clarity, direction, and a sense of purpose. It acts as a compass, helping you navigate through life's challenges with confidence. It empowers you to makedeliberate choices that lead you closer to your dreams.

"Your goals are the road maps that guide you and showyou what is possible for your life."

- Les Brown

The path that lies before us is one of transformation, empowerment, and the unwavering belief that wepossess the power to choose our priorities and shape ourdestinies. But before we delve deeper into the workings of DPS, let me share a personal story—a story that vividly illustrates the tremendous potency of speaking dreams into existence and pairing those dreams with unwavering action. This story reaffirms that dreams, when nurtured with action, have the potential to mold our reality.

Since my early years, I've held a steadfast belief in the incredible power of words to shape our reality. This beliefhas been a guiding force in my life, steering me toward a path of purpose and manifestation.

One of the most Profound keys to achieving success lies inthe remarkable ability to speak one's dreams into existence. This journey began with a simple but profound realization—one that was deeply influenced by a song that touched my soul during my high school years.

The song was "Cat's in the Cradle" by Harry Chapin, a poignant narrative about a father's evolving relationship with his son as the boy grows into a man. At its core, the song revolves around a recurring theme—an all-too-familiar tale of missed opportunities and unfulfilled promises.

In the early verses, the father's refrain echoes with an eerily familiar line: "I'm too busy right now, son, maybe later." Every time the young boy reaches out to connect with his father, to share moments and create memories, the response is the same. The father, preoccupied with life's demands, perpetually postpones those precious moments. And each time, the son's voice grows more resolute: "I'm gonna be like him, yeah, you know I'm gonna be like him."

Years pass, and the boy becomes a man. The father, now older and retired, finally finds the time he once claimed to lack. He reaches out to his grown son, eager to reconnect and share the moments he had postponed for so long. But the response he receives is unexpected and heart-wrenching. The son, now deeply engrossed in his own commitments and responsibilities, tells his father that he is too busy.

It's at this juncture that the father is struck by the profound realization that his son has indeed grown up to become just like him—too busy to seize the moments that truly matter. The poignant message of the song leaves an indelible mark, serving as a potent reminder of the consequences of our choices and priorities.

It was this song that planted the seed of a profound question within me: Could we intentionally shape our livesby positioning our dreams and priorities differently? Couldwe learn from the lessons of "Cat's in the Cradle" and proactively guide the course of our existence?

These questions ignited a journey of exploration, self-discovery, and research that ultimately led to the creation of the Dream Positioning System (DPS). This system is notjust a collection of strategies; it's a holistic approach to living a life aligned with one's dreams and aspirations.

As we delve deeper into the chapters of this book, we willunlock the secrets of DPS—strategies and principles that empower you to speak your dreams into existence, to prioritize what truly matters, and to bridge the gap between your intentions and your reality.

The Dream Positioning System is not a promise of a life without challenges or sacrifices, for those are the fibers ofthe human experience. Instead, it is a guide—a compass—that will help you navigate the complexities of life while keeping your dreams in clear view.

The journey ahead is one of transformation,empowerment, and the unwavering belief that we can indeed choose our priorities and shape our destinies. So, let us embark on this remarkable odyssey together as weunlock the full potential of the Dream Positioning Systemand chart a course toward a life that echoes with the fulfillment of our dreams.

In the wake of my encounter with "Cats in the Cradle," I found myself playing that song repeatedly, yearning to liveits message for all the right reasons. My desire was clear:I wanted to build a family that would aspire to emulate menot out of obligation but because they cherished the moments that truly mattered.

Years drifted by, and the song gradually faded from my thoughts.

Life moved forward, and I had a family of my own. And then, during my youngest son's high school years, we embarked on a remarkable journey together. We crisscrossed the country as he pursued his dream of playing college football, and I witnessed his dedication and determination on the field with immense pride.

Then, out of the blue, my son approached me with a revelation. He declared, "Dad, I've figured it out. I want tojoin the military. More specifically, I want to join the Air Force. I WANT TO BE JUST LIKE YOU!"

Those words struck a chord deep within me. I had almost forgotten about the song "Cats in the Cradle," yet my intentions and actions were still aligned with the aspiration to nurture a loving family—a family that my children would want to emulate. It was only a matter of time before my son began to reflect the qualities, he admired in me.

Today, my children truly do resemble me in many ways, and I remain committed to setting a positive example for them to follow. This story serves as a testament to the idea that speaking your dreams into existence is a critical step toward achieving your goals.

However, it's crucial to understand that dreams and goals, no matter how passionately spoken, remain incomplete without action. Consider another story from my life, whichillustrates the equation:

Speaking Dreams into Existence +Action = Success.

Those words warmed my heart in a wayI can hardly describe. I had almost forgotten about that song, but I had put my desire into the universe, and, more importantly, I had continued to work towards creating a loving relationship with my children. It was just a matter of time before my son reflected the qualities, he admired in me.

Today, my children are indeed very much like me, and I remain committed to setting a good example for them to follow. This story serves as a testament to the notion that speaking your dreams into existence is a critical aspect of accomplishing your goals.

DPS offers a promise—a promise that, with dedication, commitment, and the systematic application of its principles, you can turn your dreams into tangible, lived experiences. It's a promise that you have within you the potential to achieve more than you ever imagined.

In the chapters that follow, we will dive deep into each component of DPS. We will explore how to identify and nurture your dreams, strategically position yourself for success, and implement a systematic approach to achieve your aspirations. Through practical exercises, real-life examples, and timeless wisdom, you will be equipped with the tools and mindset needed to embark on your journey toward manifesting your dreams.

But before we proceed, take a moment to reflect on your own dreams. What do you aspire to achieve in life? As we embark on this transformative journey together, remember that your dreams are not mere fantasies—they are the seeds of your potential. DPS is here to help you nurture those seeds and watch them bloom into reality.

"Dreams are the blueprints of our soul's desires. With unwavering determination, we can turn these dreams into reality."

- Daisaku Ikeda

CHAPTER 2

THE POWER OF VISUALIZATIONAND BELIEF

"You must see the picture clearly in your mind beforeyou can turn it into reality."
- Deepak Chopra

In the realm of manifesting dreams, there exists a potent force—an invisible but transformative power that can shape the course of your life. It is a force that has been harnessed by visionaries, athletes, and entrepreneurs alike. This force is none other than the dynamic duo of Visualization and Belief.

Effective Visualization:

At its core, visualization is the practice of creating vivid mental images of your desired outcomes. It is a process that engages your imagination and taps into the immense power of your mind. Visualization is not mere daydreaming; it is a deliberate and focused mental exercise. To appreciate the power of visualization, wemust first delve into the science behind it. The brain, as a remarkable and complex organ, is responsible for processing an enormous amount of information everysecond. Among its many functions, the brain serves as the command center for your body, guiding your actions and responses. When you engage in visualization, your brain interprets these mental images as real experiences. Itactivates the same neural pathways that would be engaged if you were physically performing the actions you're visualizing. In essence, your brain cannot distinguish between a vividly imagined scenario and reality. Consider this: athletes who visualize their performances often experience improvements in theiractual physical abilities. Why? Because their brain has already "practiced" the skill through visualization. The brain is a powerful instrument that can be harnessed to your advantage.

To harness the power of visualization effectively, begin by identifying a specific goal or dream you want to manifest.It could be anything from achieving a successful career tofinding the ideal life partner. The key is to have a clear andwell-defined objective. Find a peaceful environment where you can focus without distractions. Close your eyes and take a few deep breaths to center yourself. Visualize your desired outcome in as much detail as possible. Engage all your senses. What do you see, hear, feel, smell,and taste. It's essential to infuse your visualization with the emotions you would feel if your dream were already areality. Emotions add depth and intensity to your mental imagery. Practice visualization regularly. Compile images, words, and symbols that represent your dreams and goals.Place them on a vision board and display it in a prominentplace where you can see it daily. This serves as a visual reminder of your aspirations. Imagine yourself one year, five years, or even a decade from now, having achieved your dreams. Write a letter to your future self-describing your life as you envision it. Be detailed and specific. Develop a list of positive affirmations that counteractlimiting beliefs. Repeat these affirmations daily to reinforce your belief in your abilities and potential. Set aside time each day for a guided visualization meditation.There are many resources available that can lead youthrough this process. Visualize your goals with clarity andconviction. Keep a journal to track your progress, celebrate small victories, and reflect on the ways in whichyour beliefs and visualizations are influencing youractions. more you repeat the process, the more deeply ingrained the images and emotions become in your subconscious mind. Don't limit your visualization to the result. Also, visualize the steps you'll take to get there. See yourself overcoming challenges, making progress, and ultimately achieving your goal.

Visualization alone is a powerful tool, but when coupled with unwavering belief, its effects are amplifiedexponentially. Belief is the unwavering conviction thatwhat you're visualizing is not only possible but inevitable.It's the unshakable faith in your ability to achieve your dreams.

The Role of Belief:

Belief shapes your actions and decisions. When you genuinely believe in your ability to achieve a particular outcome, you are more likely to take the necessary steps to make it a reality. Belief provides the fuel that propels you forward, even in the face of challenges. Consider the example of two individuals with identical dreams—a dream of starting a successful business. One believes wholeheartedly in their ability to achieve this dream, while the other doubts their capabilities. The firstindividual is more likely to take calculated risks, persist through setbacks, and seek out opportunities. Their beliefin success drives their actions.

While belief is a potent force, it's important to recognize that not all beliefs serve your best interests. Limiting beliefs, often acquired through past experiences or external influences, can hinder your progress. These beliefs may include notions like "I'm not good enough" or"Success is only for others." Overcoming limiting beliefs isa critical step in harnessing the full power of belief in yourjourney to manifest your dreams. To do so, you must challenge and replace these negative beliefs with positive, empowering ones. This process can be achieved through self-reflection, self-affirmation, and seeking support from mentors and resources.

Visualization, in its essence, is the art of painting thecanvas of possibility with the colors of belief. It requires usto close our eyes and see our dreams not as distant fantasies but as achievable realities. Imagine, for a moment, the dream you hold closest to your heart. See itin intricate detail—the sights, the sounds, the emotions. Imagine it with such clarity that it feels as real as the world you currently inhabit. This is the starting point of transformation, for what we can envision with unwavering belief, we can manifest.

In the interplay of visualization and belief, we find the synergy that transforms dreams into accomplishments. Itis not enough to dream, nor is it sufficient to act without direction. The true power resides in combining the two—the clear vision of what we desire and the audacity to acton that hope.

As we journey through this chapter, we will explore techniques for effective visualization, strategies for nurturing unwavering belief, and the transformative impact of aligning our thoughts with our actions. Together, we will unlock the potential within us to turn dreams into tangible, extraordinary realities.

Walt Disney, the creative genius behind Disneyland and the Disney empire, faced numerous rejections andsetbacks on his path to success. Yet, he never wavered in his belief in the power of dreams. Disney famously said, "All our dreams can come true if we have the courage to pursue them."

His unwavering belief in the magic of imagination and the potential for dreams to become reality transformed the entertainment industry and continues to inspire generations.

The power of visualization and belief cannot be overstated. They are the keys to unlocking your potential and manifesting your dreams.

"Visualizing your desired outcome is the first step toward bringing it to life."

- Carlos Castaneda

CHAPTER 3

UNLOCKING YOUR INNER POTENTIAL

"The potential for greatness resides within each of us. It is our responsibility to unlock it."

- Daisaku Ikeda

Your journey towards manifesting your dreams begins with understanding and unlocking your inner potential. It's a profound and transformative process that involves self-discovery, self-belief, and the courage to tap into the boundless capabilities within you. In this chapter, we'll delve deep into the essence of unlocking your inner potential.

Cultivating Your Potential

Unlocking your inner potential is the process of discovering, nurturing, and harnessing your innate abilities, talents, and capabilities to their fullest extent. It involves recognizing the untapped resources within yourself and taking deliberate actions to bring them to the forefront. It starts with getting to know yourself better. This involves introspection, self-reflection, and gaining a deep understanding of your strengths, weaknesses, passions, values, and beliefs. To unlock your potential, you must first believe in your abilities and have confidence in your capacity to learn and grow. Self-belief is the foundation upon which all further progress is built.

Identifying your goals and aspirations provides direction and purpose. Clear, well-defined goals serve as roadmaps for your journey toward unlocking your potential. Embrace a growth mindset and remain open to learning new skills and acquiring knowledge. Lifelong learning is essential for personal development. Growth often occurs when you step out of your comfort zone. Embracing challenges and facing adversity can help you discover new facets of your potential. Overcoming obstacles and setbacks in essence, unlocking your inner potential is an ongoing, transformative journey of self-discovery and self-improvement. It involves recognizing the boundless possibilities within yourself and taking deliberate steps to harness them, ultimately leading to personal growth, fulfillment, and the realization of your dreams and aspirations.

Finding your life's purpose is vitally important for unlocking your inner potential because it provides a clear and meaningful direction for your personal growth and development. When you discover your life's purpose, you gain a clear sense of what truly matters to you. This clarity allows you to focus your time, energy, and resources on pursuits that align with your purpose, reducing distractions and wasted efforts. Your life's purpose is often linked to your passions and interests. When you engage in activities that resonate with your purpose, you naturally feel more motivated and enthusiastic. This intrinsic motivation propels you to put in the effort needed to unlock your potential. Knowing your life's purpose provides a strong sense of meaning and fulfillment. During challenging times, this sense of purpose acts as a source of resilience. It helps you bounce back from setbacks and stay committed to your personal growth journey. Discovering your life's purpose involves deep self-exploration and self-awareness. This process allows you to better understand your strengths, values, and beliefs. Self-discovery is a fundamental step in unlocking your inner potential. Your life's purpose is often closely tied to your core values. Living in alignment with your values brings a sense of authenticity and integrity. This alignment enhances your personal growth efforts by ensuring they are in harmony with your true self. A clear life purpose serves as a guiding principle for setting meaningful goals. Goals that are aligned with your purpose are more likely to inspire you, leading to greater dedication and persistence in achieving them. When you live in alignment with your life's purpose, you tend to attract like-minded individuals who share similar values and passions. Building relationships with people who resonate with your purpose can provide support and collaboration opportunities in your personal growthjourney. Your life's purpose is not static; it evolves as you grow and change. Embracing personal growth becomes anongoing process as you continually align your actions withyour evolving purpose. Ultimately, finding and living your life's purpose leads to a deep sense of fulfillment and contentment. This sense of fulfillment is a powerful motivator to continue exploring your potential andpursuing your dreams. Your life's purpose acts as a guidingstar, illuminating the path to unlocking your inner potential. It gives meaning to your actions, fuels yourmotivation, and helps you navigate the challenges of personal growth. When you are in tune with your life's purpose, you are more likely to realize your full potential and live a fulfilling, purpose-driven life.

Overcoming self-doubt and fear is often necessary when unlocking your inner potential. Self-doubt and fear often stem from self-limiting beliefs. These are negative beliefs about your abilities, worthiness, or potential. These beliefs can hold you back from taking risks and pursuing opportunities that could lead to personal growth. Fear of failure or making mistakes can make you risk-averse. However, taking calculated risks is often necessary for personal growth. When you allow fear to dictate your actions, you may miss out on valuable learning experiences and opportunities for advancement. Self- doubt and fear can keep you stuck in your comfort zone. While it may feel safe, the comfort zone is where personal growth stagnates. Unlocking your inner potential requires stepping outside of this zone and embracing new challenges. Fear and self-doubt can lead to self-sabotaging behaviors. You might procrastinate, avoid acting, or engage in negative self-talk. These behaviors can undermine your progress and potential. Self-doubt erodesself-confidence, which is crucial for pursuing goals and realizing your potential. Confidence empowers you to take on challenges, persevere through setbacks, and believe in your ability to learn and grow. When you allow self-doubt and fear to control your decisions, you may miss opportunities for personal development. These opportunities could include pursuing a new career path, learning a new skill, or taking on leadership roles. Unlocking your inner potential often involves self- exploration and pushing your boundaries. Overcoming self-doubt and fear allows you to explore your capabilities, strengths, and weaknesses more fully. Building resilience is a key aspect of personal growth. When you overcome self-doubt and fear, you develop the resilience to bounceback from failures and setbacks. This resilience is essentialfor long-term personal development. Overcoming self- doubt and fear contributes to developing a more positiveself-image. As you build confidence and face your fears, you start to see yourself as capable and resilient, which can further fuel your personal growth. Achieving yourgoals and realizing your potential often requires pushing through self-doubt and fear. Whether it's pursuing a dream career, starting a business, or excelling in a new skill, facing these obstacles is part of the journey. While self-doubt and fear are common obstacles in the path to unlocking your inner potential, they are not insurmountable. Overcoming these challenges is an essential part of personal growth and development. By addressing self-doubt and fear head-on, you can gain the confidence and resilience needed to reach your full potential and lead a more fulfilling life.

Continuous Learning and Growth

Continuous learning is of paramount importance when it comes to unlocking your inner potential. In our rapidly evolving world, change is constant. Continuous learning equips you with the knowledge and skills needed to adapt to new circumstances, technologies, and challenges. It enables you to thrive in an ever-changing environment, unlocking your potential to excel in various situations. Learning is a catalyst for personal growth. When you engage in continuous learning, you challenge yourself to acquire new knowledge and skills. This process not only expands your capabilities but also enhances your self- esteem and confidence. It encourages you to step out of your comfort zone and explore your potential. Learning exposes you to diverse perspectives, ideas, and cultures. It broadens your horizons and encourages open- mindedness. This expanded worldview can enrich your personal and professional life, enabling you to connect with others on a deeper level and fostering personal growth. Continuous learning sharpens your problem- solving abilities. It equips you with a broader toolkit of strategies and approaches for addressing challenges. As you tackle new problems and acquire fresh knowledge, you become more effective at overcoming obstacles and unlocking your inner potential. Learning fuels innovation. It encourages you to think creatively and develop innovative solutions. By staying up to date with emerging trends and technologies, you can harness your creativity to achieve new heights in your personal and professional endeavors. Continuous learners tend to be more resilient. They view setbacks and failures as opportunities for growth rather than insurmountable obstacles. This resilience is a critical trait for unlocking your inner potential because it allows you to bounce back from setbacks and keep moving forward. In today's competitive job market, continuous learning is a key factor in career advancement. Acquiring new skills and knowledge can make you a more valuable asset to your organization or open doors to new career opportunities. It allows you to tap into your full potential and reach your professional goals. As you accumulate knowledge and expertise through continuous learning, your confidence grows. Thisself-assuredness is vital for unlocking your inner potential. It empowers you to pursue ambitious goals, take on leadership roles, and navigate challenges with poise. Studies suggest that lifelong learning can contribute to cognitive health and longevity. By keeping your mind engaged and active, you may reduce the risk of cognitive decline as you age. This cognitive fitness is essential for maintaining your ability to explore and develop your inner potential throughout your life. Learning is not just a meansto an end; it's a source of personal fulfillment. Continuous learning allows you to pursue your interests, passions, andcuriosities. It fosters a sense of purpose and excitement about life, motivating you to unlock your inner potential with enthusiasm. Continuous learning is an indispensablecomponent of unlocking your inner potential. Itempowers you to adapt, grow, and thrive in an ever-changing world. By embracing a lifelong learning mindset, you can harness your full capabilities, achieve personal and professional success, and lead a fulfilling life.

Cultivating resilience is crucial for unlocking your inner potential for several reasons. It enables you to view challenges as opportunities for growth rather thaninsurmountable obstacles. When you encounter setbacks or face adversity, a resilient mindset helps you maintain apositive outlook and the belief that you can overcome difficulties. It fosters the ability to persevere. It helps you stay committed to your goals and aspirations, even in theface of adversity or temporary failures. This determinationis essential for unlocking your inner potential, as it keeps you on the path to success despite obstacles. Resilient individuals are flexible and adaptable. They can adjust their strategies and approach when faced with changing circumstances. This adaptability is crucial for harnessing your inner potential because it allows you to navigate different situations and seize opportunities as they arise. Resiliency equips you with effective stress management skills. When you can handle stress and pressure in a healthy way, you're better able to focus your energy on personal growth and development. Stress reduction is essential for unlocking your potential, as chronic stress can impede progress and enhances problem-solving abilities. It encourages you to approach challenges with a creative and constructive mindset, seeking solutions rather than dwelling on problems. Effective problem-solving is a key component of personal growth and unlocking your potential. Individuals tend to maintain a more optimistic outlook. This positive attitude can fuel your motivation and determination to achieve your goals. When you believe in a brighter future, you're more likely to take actions that lead to personal growth. Additionally, overcoming obstacles through resilience builds self-confidence. When you face adversity and come out stronger on the other side, you gain confidence in your abilities. This self-assuredness is vital for unlocking your inner potential, as it encourages you to tackle new challenges. It provides you with the courage to take calculated risks. To unlock your potential, you often need to step out of your comfort zone and embrace new opportunities. A resilient mindset reduces the fear of failure, making you more willing to take risks that can lead to personal growth and contributes to healthy relationships. Your ability to bounce back from setbacks and maintain a positive attitude can inspire and uplift those around you. Positive relationships can provide support and encouragement on your journey to unlocking your potential. Resiliency is closely linked to emotional well-being. When you cultivate resilience, you're better equipped to manage negative emotions and maintain a sense of inner peace. Emotional well-being is a foundation for personal growth and realizing your potential. Cultivating resilience is essential for unlocking your inner potential because it empowers you to face challenges, persevere in the pursuit of your goals, adapt to changing circumstances, and maintain a positive mindset. With resilience, you're better equipped to navigate the ups anddowns of life's journey and fully explore your capabilities and potential for growth.

Surrounding yourself with support is crucial when unlocking your inner potential. Supportive individuals provide encouragement and motivation. They believe in your abilities and aspirations, boosting your confidence and determination. Their positive reinforcement can inspire you to take action toward unlocking your potential.

When you have a support system, you're more likely to beheld accountable for your goals and actions. Knowing thatothers are invested in your success encourages you to staycommitted and responsible for your personal growth. Support often comes from individuals who have already achieved personal growth and success in areas relevant toyour goals. They can offer valuable guidance, share their experiences, and serve as mentors. Learning from their insights can accelerate your journey toward unlocking your potential. Your support network can provide access to knowledge and resources that you may not have on your own. Whether it's books, courses, connections, or tools, these resources can be instrumental in your personal development efforts. Supportive friends, mentors, or coaches can offer constructive feedback and a fresh perspective on your progress. They can help you identify blind spots, offer solutions to challenges, and provide honest assessments that guide your growth. Having a support system contributes to your emotional well-being. Knowing that you have people who care aboutyour success can reduce stress and anxiety. Emotional stability is essential for maintaining focus and resilience on your journey.

Being around supportive individuals who are also pursuing their goals can be highly inspiring. Witnessing their achievements and determination can motivate you to strive for more and continue your path toward unlocking your potential. Collaboration with supportive peers can lead to synergistic efforts. Together, you can work on shared goals, exchange ideas, and create opportunities that may not be achievable alone.

Collaboration can accelerate your personal growth. When you share your goals and progress with your support system, it creates a sense of accountability. This accountability encourages consistency in your actions, as you're more likely to follow through on your commitments. On your journey to unlocking your inner potential, you will encounter obstacles and setbacks. Having a support network means you're not facing these challenges alone. Your supporters can help you overcome obstacles by offering solutions, perspective, or simply being there to listen. Your support system celebrates your achievements with you. Sharing your successes with others who genuinely appreciate your efforts provides a sense of fulfillment and encourages you to set new goals and continue growing. Surrounding yourself with support is essential for unlocking your inner potential because it provides encouragement, motivation, guidance, and access to valuable resources. It helps you stay accountable, maintain emotional well-being, and navigate challenges more effectively. With a support network, you're better equipped to achieve your personal growth goals and reach your full potential.

Each one of us possesses a reservoir of untapped potential. This potential encompasses talents, abilities, creativity, and strengths that often lie dormant or undiscovered. It's the part of you that has yet to be fully expressed and utilized. To comprehend the concept of potential fully, consider it as a vast field of possibilities. It's the uncharted territory within you where new skills can be developed, fresh ideas can sprout, and your best self can emerge. This potential is not limited by age, circumstances, or past experiences. It remains ever- present, waiting for you to unlock its treasures. Realizing your inner potential is like discovering hidden treasures within yourself. When you unlock your potential, you experience a profound sense of fulfillment, purpose, and achievement. You become more resilient in the face of challenges, and your capacity to create, innovate, and influence grows exponentially.

Your potential isn't just about personal success; it also enables you to make a positive impact on the world. By fully utilizing your abilities, you can contribute to thebetterment of society, inspire others, and leave a lasting legacy.

Unlocking your inner potential begins with a journey of self-discovery. It involves exploring the depths of your being to understand who you are, what you value, and what drives you. Self-discovery is not a one-time event; it'san ongoing process of introspection and growth.

Know Thyself

It's important to "Know Thyself". Know and recognizeyour values are the principles that guide your life. Take time to identify your core values—those beliefs that are most important to you. Aligning your actions with your values is a key to unlocking your potential. What are yournatural talents and abilities? Reflect on the activities that come easily to you and bring you joy. Understanding yourstrengths allows you to leverage them to achieve your dreams. Knowing and accepting your Passion is the driving force behind your potential. What activities or causes ignite your enthusiasm? Exploring your passions can lead to fulfilling pursuits aligned with your dreams. Be aware, fear often holds us back from realizing our potential. Identify your fears and confront them. Overcoming fear is a significant step toward unlocking your inner potential. Setting Goals gives you direction and purpose. Define clear and inspiring goals that reflect your values, strengths, and passions. These goals will serve as milestones on your journey.

"You don't become what you want, you become what you believe."

- Oprah Winfrey

CHAPTER 4

SETTING CLEAR ANDINSPIRING GOALS

"Goals are the fuel in the furnace of achievement."
- Brian Tracy

Goals are like signposts on the road to success. Theydefine the path, keep you focused, and measure your progress. Understanding the power of goals is the first step in harnessing their potential. Goals serve as powerfulmotivators. They ignite your passion and drive. When youhave a clear, inspiring goal, you are more likely to persevere through challenges and setbacks. Your goal becomes a source of energy that propels you forward. A well-defined goal brings clarity to your aspirations. It answers the "what" and "why" of your journey. When youarticulate your goals, you create a mental image of your desired destination. This clarity allows you to stay focusedon the actions that will lead you there. Goal setting is theact of defining your desired outcomes and creating aroadmap to reach them. It's the bridge between yourdreams and their realization.

Goals provide a yardstick to measure your progress. Theyallow you to track your achievements, celebrate successes, and make necessary adjustments along the way. This measurement helps you stay on course and maintain momentum. To set goals that have a profound impact on your journey they must be specific. They leave no room for ambiguity. Instead of saying, "I want to be successful," specify what success means to you. For example, "I want to earn $100,000 in annual income" is aspecific goal. They need to be measurable. Goals allow youto track your progress objectively. You should be able to quantify and measure your achievements. Instead of a vague goal like "improve my health," a measurable goal would be "lose 20 pounds in six months." Goals should bechallenging but attainable. Setting goals that are too lofty can lead to frustration and demotivation. Assess your capabilities and resources realistically. For instance, if you're starting a business, aiming for a 200% profit increase in a month might not be achievable and goals should align with your dreams, values, and aspirations. Ensure that your goals are relevant to your overall vision.Pursuing goals that resonate with your core desires fuels your passion and commitment. Set deadlines for yourgoals is also necessary. A time-bound goal creates a senseof urgency and prevents procrastination. Without a timeline, your goal lacks the structure necessary for achievement. For instance, "write a book in one year" is atime-bound goal.

Goals are not set in stone. They should be adaptable to changing circumstances. Be open to adjusting your goals if needed while staying true to your ultimate vision. Celebrating milestones along your journey is crucial for maintaining motivation. Acknowledge your achievements, no matter how small. Each step forward brings you closerto your goal.

Effective goal setting involves a structured process that ensures your goals are well-defined and aligned with yourdreams. Begin by revisiting your dreams and aspirations. What do you truly desire in life? Reflect on your long-termvision. Your goals should reflect your dreams. Divide yourlong-term vision into shorter-term goals. Break them down into smaller, manageable steps. These smaller goalsserve as milestones on your journey. Big goals can sometimes seem overwhelming. To make them manageable, break them into smaller, achievable steps. This approach, often referred to as "chunking," whichensures that you maintain focus and motivation along theway. In my upcoming book "The 24-Hour

Millionaire", I will do a deep dive into the importance of breaking long-term goals into small bite size daily tasks. Not all goals are created equal. Prioritize your goals based on theirimportance and urgency. Focus on one or a few primary goals at a time to avoid spreading yourself too thin. Putting your goals in writing solidifies your commitment. Use positive language and present tense when writing your goals. For example, "I am earning $100,000 annually by December 31, 20XX." Identify the actions and steps required to achieve each goal. Your action plan should outline the specific tasks, resources, and timelines neededfor success. Visualization is a powerful tool in goal setting. Regularly visualize yourself achieving your goals with clarity and emotion. This reinforces your commitment andbelief in their attainment and regularly review your goals to track progress. Celebrate your achievements and adjust your strategies if necessary. Sometimes, circumstances change, and your goals may need to adapt accordingly.

Visualization is a powerful tool for goal setting. By vividly imagining your success, you enhance your belief in your ability to achieve your goals.

Passion is the fuel that sustains your journey toward yourgoals. When you set goals that align with your passions, you infuse your actions with enthusiasm and energy. Passion transforms the pursuit of goals from a chore into a fulfilling endeavor. To harness the power of passion in goal setting, identify what truly excites and motivates you.What activities, causes, or pursuits bring you joy and fulfillment? Align your goals with these passions. Passion helps you navigate challenges with resilience. When you encounter obstacles on your path, your passion for your goals acts as a source of determination and perseverance.More importantly, you should understand, passion is contagious. When you pursue your goals with enthusiasmand commitment, you inspire others to do the same. Yourpassion can create a ripple effect of positive change. Inspiration is the fuel that propels you toward your goals. Your goals should resonate deeply with your values and passions.

Elon Musk, the visionary entrepreneur behind SpaceX andTesla, has set an inspiring goal to make humanity a multi-planetary species. His vision is to establish a human settlement on Mars. This audacious goal has ignited passion and innovation in the field of space exploration, pushing the boundaries of what's possible.

Nelson Mandela's goal of ending apartheid and achievingfreedom and equality in South Africa inspired a nation andthe world. His commitment to this goal led to his enduringlegacy as a symbol of hope, reconciliation, and justice.

A close friend of mine named Joni Redick' wrote a book called, "Million Dollar Attitude," she introduces us to the transformative power of mindset. At the heart of herteachings is the notion that our attitude toward our goalsand dreams profoundly influences their attainment. She champions the belief that adopting a million-dollarattitude is not reserved for the elite; it is a mindset accessible to all who dare to dream. Her wisdom remindsus that our goals are not merely destinations; they are reflections of our innermost desires. To set clear andinspiring goals, we must first cultivate a mindset that radiates positivity, resilience, and unwavering determination. It is this attitude that propels us forward, even in the face of adversity, and compels us to dream big.In the realm of setting clear and inspiring goals, we find a fusion of attitude and vision.

To set and achieve inspiring goals effectively, create a vision board that visually represents your goals and dreams. Use images, words, and symbols that resonate with your aspirations. Place it where you can see it daily to stay motivated. Keep a journal dedicated to your goals.Write down your goals, action plans, and progress. Use this journal for reflection and to celebrate your achievements.

Accountability is essential for staying on track with your goals. Share your goals with someone you trust who can hold you accountable. Additionally, track your progress tostay motivated.

Create empowering and inspiring affirmations for yourself.

I came to realize that my name is an affirmation, one thatspeaks to me every day and every second of my life, "David B. Rich"!! Be Rich in Love, Wealth, Passion and Compassion. Be Rich in Giving and Be Rich in Happiness and most importantly, Be Spiritually Rich!

Another Daily Affirmation that continues to inspire and create space in my life is one I have recited for many years:

- Today I dedicate my life to Kosen Rufu (World Peace)

- To be so strong that nothing can upset the peace ofthis of my mind

- To talk of health happiness and hope to every personI meet

- To make my friends feel that there's something goodand beautiful in them

- To look at the sunny side of everything and to be optimistic about Life

- To think only the best - work toward doing and experiencing only the best

- To be just as happy about the success of others as I amabout my own success

- To forgive my mistakes of the past and press forwardto greater achievements in the future

- To give so much time to improve myself that I have notime to criticize others.

- To be too strong for fear, too kind for anger, and too happy for worry.

- To lift my heart in faith each day so that theGohonzon* will be so forth in my life.

In conclusion, setting clear and inspiring goals is a transformative process that requires clarity, inspiration, adaptability, and accountability. Your goals serve as the guiding stars on your journey towards manifesting your dreams. As Antoine de Saint-Exupéry aptly said, "A goal without a plan is just a wish."

Your potential is boundless, and your goals are the steppingstones to realizing it. Remember that your goals are not just destinations; they are the means to a fulfillingand purpose-driven life. Embrace the power of purposeful goal setting, and watch as your dreams come to life, one goal at a time.

Finally, don't hesitate to seek support and collaborate with others who share your goals. As Helen Keller remarked, "Alone we can do so little; together we can do so much."

"Whatever the mind can conceive and believe,it can achieve."
- Napoleon Hill

* Gohonzon is a spiritual Mandela that SGI Buddhist practitioners chant toward for internal spiritual direction, clarity, and happiness. The Gohonzon is a scroll containing Chinese and Sanskrit characters that aids practitioners of Nichiren Buddhism in the process of perceiving and bringing forth the life condition of Buddhahood from within their lives.

CHAPTER 5

CREATING YOUR PERSONALDREAM BLUEPRINT

"The best way to predict the future is to create it."
- Peter Drucker

Imagine your life as a magnificent work of art, waiting to be painted. A Personal Dream Blueprint is your canvas—acarefully crafted plan that outlines your aspirations, desires, and goals. In this chapter, we will explore what a Personal Dream Blueprint is, how to create one, and why it's essential in the journey to manifest your dreams. Through relatable examples, historical stories, scientific insights, and inspiring quotes, we'll unveil the power of this transformative tool.

A Personal Dream Blueprint is a detailed and dynamic roadmap that defines your life's vision, values, and goals. It's not just a list of objectives but a comprehensive plan that aligns with your deepest desires and ambitions. As Earl Nightingale once said, "People with goals succeed because they know where they're going."

Imagine, for instance, a young Thomas Edison sketching his blueprint for inventing the phonograph. His vision wasclear: to capture and reproduce sound. Edison's blueprint was not merely about invention; it was a manifestation ofhis passion for audio innovation.

The Blueprint for Success

Your Personal Dream Blueprint begins with self-discovery.Reflect on your values, strengths, passions, and purpose. This step is akin to sketching the outline of your masterpiece. A Personal Dream Blueprint requires a strategic plan that breaks down your goals into actionablesteps. It's like mixing the paints and selecting the brushesfor your masterpiece. Your blueprint should allow for adaptability, much like adjusting brush strokes to refine apainting. Life's twists and turns may require alterations toyour plan. Great works of art often have mentors and collaborators behind them. Seek guidance, support, and inspiration from those who share your vision.

A Personal Dream Blueprint provides clarity in a world filled with distractions. It serves as your compass, helpingyou stay focused on your chosen path. As Brian Tracy noted, "Goals allow you to control the direction of changein your favor." During challenging times, your blueprint becomes your source of motivation and resilience. It reminds you why you started and encourages you to persevere. As Winston Churchill said, "Success is not final,failure is not fatal: it is the courage to continue that counts." Having a blueprint streamlines decision-making and enhances efficiency. It prevents wasted energy on pursuits that do not align with your vision. It's akin to following a well-constructed recipe for success. Your blueprint allows you to measure your progress and celebrate milestones. Each completed goal is a stroke of accomplishment on your canvas of dreams.

NASA's Apollo program aimed to land humans on themoon. This monumental achievement had a meticulouslycrafted blueprint, outlining spacecraft design, mission objectives, and astronaut training. The blueprint ensured that each Apollo mission was built upon the previous one, leading to the historic lunar landing in 1969.

A dream blueprint is akin to architectural plans for a grandbuilding. It outlines the design, structure, and execution ofyour dreams. It transforms abstract desires into concrete goals and action steps. Begin by revisiting your dreams and desires. What do you want to achieve in various areas of your life—career, relationships, personal development, health, and more? Clarity about your dreams is essential, as it serves as the foundation for your blueprint.

Not all dreams are equally urgent or important. Prioritize them based on their significance to your overall happiness and fulfillment. Which dreams are you most passionate about and eager to pursue? Divide your goals into manageable, smaller steps. These become the action items on your blueprint. Breaking down your goals makes them less overwhelming and more achievable. For each step, outline the specific actions, resources, and timelinesrequired. Your action plan serves as your day-to-day guide. It details what needs to be done and by when. In addition to the goal, establish milestones or checkpoints along the way. These are like rest stops on your journey, allowing you to assess your progress and celebrate achievements. Regularly engage in visualization exerciseswhere you see yourself accomplishing your goals withclarity and emotion. Visualization reinforces your belief inthe attainability of your dreams. Regularly review your dream blueprint. Assess your progress and adjust as necessary. Life is dynamic, and circumstances may change, requiring you to adapt your plan. Accountability isa powerful tool in the execution of your dream blueprint.When you share your goals and progress with someone else—a friend, family member, mentor, or coach— you create a sense of responsibility to follow through. They can provide encouragement, support, and feedback, keeping you on track. Consider partnering with someone who can hold you accountable for your goals. Regular check-ins and discussions about your progress can behighly motivating. Choose someone you trust and who shares your enthusiasm for your dreams. Maintain a record of your achievements and setbacks. Tracking your progress not only holds you accountable but also helps you identify patterns, learn from experiences, and make informed adjustments to your dream blueprint.

As you pursue your dreams through your dream blueprint, you are likely to encounter challenges and obstacles alongthe way. These hurdles are a natural part of the journey, and they provide opportunities for growth and learning. Resilience is the ability to bounce back from setbacks. When facing challenges, remind yourself of your passion and commitment to your dreams. Embrace setbacks as learning experiences and continue moving forward. Don'thesitate to seek support and resources when facing challenges. Whether it's guidance from a mentor, new skills through education, or additional research, there areoften ways to overcome obstacles with the right assistance. Your dream blueprint should be flexible. As circumstances change, be prepared to adjust your plan while keeping your ultimate dreams in sight. Adaptability is a valuable trait on the path to success. Maintain agrowth mindset throughout your journey. Embrace challenges as opportunities to develop your skills andcharacter. A positive mindset is a powerful asset in overcoming obstacles.

As you work diligently toward your dreams, it's important to maintain a healthy work-life balance. Achieving your dreams should enhance your overall well-being, not compromise it. Make self-care a non-negotiable part of your routine. This includes physical health, mental well- being, and emotional balance. Regular exercise, adequate rest, and mindfulness practices contribute to your resilience and productivity. Establish clear boundaries between your work, personal life, and pursuit of dreams. Allocate dedicated time for each aspect of your life to prevent burnout and maintain harmony. Don't hesitate to delegate tasks or seek assistance when needed. Whetherit's in your career or personal life, recognizing when you need support is a sign of strength. Effective time management is crucial. Prioritize tasks based on theirimportance and deadlines. Use tools like calendars and to- do lists to stay organized and focused. Celebrate your achievements, both big and small. Recognize your progress and reward yourself for your hard work.

Celebration adds motivation and enjoyment to your journey.

To create your personal dream blueprint effectively, maintain a journal dedicated to your dreams and aspirations. Write down your long-term vision and specific goals. Use this journal for regular reflections and updates.Create a visual mind map of your dreams and goals. This graphical representation can help you see the connectionsbetween different aspects of your life and your overarching dreams.

In conclusion, a Personal Dream Blueprint is your personalized guide to manifesting your dreams. It's a dynamic plan rooted in self-discovery, clear goals, adaptability, and support. Much like a masterpiece inprogress, your life's canvas awaits your inspired strokes. With a well-crafted blueprint, you can turn your dreams into a reality that reflects your truest desires and aspirations.

"The future depends on what you do today."
- Mahatma Gandhi

CHAPTER 6

OVERCOMING LIMITINGBELIEFS AND FEARS

"Your beliefs create your reality. When you change yourbeliefs, you change your reality."
-Thomas Wilhite

In the journey towards manifesting your dreams with theDream Positioning System (DPS), one of the most formidable obstacles you'll encounter is the presence of limiting beliefs and fears. These mental roadblocks can belike heavy chains holding you back from reaching your fullpotential. In this chapter, we will delve deep into understanding what limiting beliefs and fears are, explore their origins, and provide effective strategies for overcoming them.

Identifying Limiting Beliefs

Limiting beliefs are deeply ingrained thoughts or convictions that constrain your actions and hinder your progress. They are often formed in childhood, influenced by experiences, family, society, or self-doubt. Limiting beliefs act as the barriers that keep you from pursuing your dreams.

Imagine a young child who's told repeatedly that they're not good enough, smart enough, or talented enough.

These negative messages can shape their beliefs about themselves, ultimately limiting their self-esteem and aspirations. These beliefs may persist into adulthood, affecting one's career, relationships, and overall happiness.

Beliefs are the lenses through which you perceive the world and your place in it. They shape your thoughts, actions, and, ultimately, your reality.

Before we delve into overcoming limiting beliefs and fears, let's recognize the incredible influence that belief holds over our lives. Belief is the lens through which we perceive the world and our own potential. It shapes our thoughts, feelings, and actions.

Belief can be a self-fulfilling prophecy. When you believe in your abilities and the possibility of success, you are more likely to take actions that lead to positive outcomes.Conversely, if you harbor limiting beliefs and doubts, your actions may reflect these negative expectations.

Many of our beliefs, both empowering and limiting, are shaped by our upbringing, experiences, and the influencesof society. These beliefs can become deeply ingrained in our subconscious minds, guiding our behavior without ourconscious awareness.

Limiting beliefs are those thoughts or convictions that undermine your self-confidence, self-worth, and belief in your abilities. They often take the form of negative self- talk or irrational fears. Identifying them is the first step toovercoming their grip on your life. They are often deeply ingrained and may stem from past experiences, societal conditioning, or self-doubt. To overcome these beliefs, you must first identify them. Reflect on the thoughts and self-talk patterns that hold you back. Journaling and self- awareness exercises can be powerful tools for uncovering limiting beliefs.

- **Self-Doubt:** Believing you are not good enough, smartenough, or capable enough to achieve your dreams.

- **Fear of Failure:** Expecting that any attempt to reach your dreams will end in failure, leading to avoidance or procrastination.

- **Perfectionism:** Believing that success can only be achieved through flawlessness, leading to paralyzing perfectionist tendencies.

- **Scarcity Mindset:** Believing that there are not enough resources, opportunities, or success to go around, leading to a sense of competition or hoarding.

- **Imposter Syndrome:** Feeling like a fraud, believing that your achievements are undeserved or due to luck rather than your abilities.

Limiting beliefs can take various forms, such as:

- **I'm not worthy:** Believing you don't deserve success or happiness.

- **I'm not capable:** Feeling inadequate and doubting your abilities.

- **I'm not lucky:** Believing that success is dependent on luck, not effort.

- **I'm too old/young:** Using age as an excuse for not pursuing dreams.

- **I'm afraid of failure:** Fear of failing is so paralyzing that it prevents action.

The Psychology of Fear

Fear is a natural human emotion that has evolved to protect us from danger. However, in the context of pursuing your dreams, fear can become a paralyzing force. It often arises from the unknown, the possibility of failure, or the fear of rejection or judgment. Some Common Fears in Achieving Dreams. Fears are closely intertwined with limiting beliefs. They are the emotional responses triggered by those beliefs. Fear can be a potent force that keeps you stuck in your comfort zone. It often manifests as:

- **Fear of failure:** The dread of failing in your endeavors.

- **Fear of rejection:** The anxiety about being criticized or rejected by others.

- **Fear of the unknown:** Apprehension about what might happen if you step out of your comfort zone.

- **Fear of change:** The resistance to embracing new experiences or challenges.

- **Fear of success:** Surprisingly, the fear of achieving your dreams and the responsibilities it might entail.

Overcoming Limiting Beliefs and Fears

Self-awareness:

The first step in overcoming limiting beliefs and fears is recognizing and acknowledging them. Self-awareness is the key to understanding the root causes of these beliefs.Reflect on your thoughts and feelings to pinpoint where these limitations stem from. Take time to introspect and explore your thoughts and feelings. Pay attention to recurring patterns of self-doubt, negativity, or fear.

Challenge and reframe:

Once identified, challenge your limiting beliefs. Challengethem with evidence to the contrary. Ask yourself if they are based on facts or assumptions. Replace negative beliefs with positive, empowering affirmations. Seek examples of people who have achieved similar dreams despite facing similar challenges or doubts. If you believe you're not capable, reframe it as "I am capable of learningand growing." Keep a journal where you write down your thoughts and feelings. This can help you identify recurringlimiting beliefs and the situations that trigger them.

Seek support:

Share your aspirations and fears with trusted friends, mentors, or a coach. They can provide guidance, encouragement, and a fresh perspective. Often, they've faced similar challenges and can offer valuable insights. Sometimes, others can recognize your limiting beliefs when you may not. Seek feedback from trusted friends, mentors, or coaches who can provide insights.

Visualization and positive imagery:

Visualization techniques can help you overcome fears. Imagine yourself succeeding, feeling confident, and conquering your obstacles. Repeatedly visualizing positiveoutcomes can gradually reshape your beliefs and reduce fear. Practices like mindfulness and meditation can increase your self-awareness and help you observe your thoughts without judgment.

Action-oriented mindset:

Take small, manageable steps towards your goals. Each achievement builds confidence and weakens limiting beliefs. Remember that even failures are opportunities tolearn and grow.

Embrace failure:

Understand that failure is a natural part of the journey tosuccess. It's not a reflection of your worth. As Thomas Edison famously said, "I have not failed. I've just found 10,000 ways that won't work." Each setback brings you closer to your dreams.

To overcome fears that hold you back from pursuing yourdreams, you must acknowledge and confront them head-on. Recognize and accept that fear is a natural emotion. It's okay to feel fear; what matters is how you respond toit. Dig deeper to understand the source of your fear. Is it afear of failure, rejection, or the unknown? Identifying theroot cause can help you address it more effectively. Change your perception of fear. Instead of seeing it as a barrier, view it as a sign that you are pushing your boundaries and growing. Visualize yourself confronting and overcoming your fears. Gradual exposure to the source of your fear, through desensitization, can also helpreduce its impact. Break down your dreams into smaller, less intimidating steps. Taking small, manageable actions can build your confidence and reduce fear.

The first step in conquering fear is acknowledging it. Avoidance and denial only reinforce fear's grip on your life. Instead, name your fears and bring them into the light. Counteract limiting beliefs and fear with positive affirmations. Create statements that challenge your negative self-talk and reinforce empowering beliefs. Visualize yourself achieving your dreams and overcoming obstacles. Visualization can reprogram your subconsciousmind to align with your goals. Associate with people who uplift and support you. Surrounding yourself with positivity can counteract the influence of negative beliefs.Expand your knowledge and skills. The more you learn andgrow, the more confident you become in your abilities to overcome challenges. Acknowledge and celebrate your achievements, no matter how small they may seem. Each success reinforces your belief in your capabilities. Changeyour perspective on failure. Instead of viewing it as a setback, see it as an opportunity to learn and grow. Keep a journal to track your progress in overcoming limiting beliefs and fears. Reflect on your experiences and insights.

Before becoming a household name with Harry Potter, J.K.Rowling faced rejection from multiple publishers. She overcame her fear of failure and persisted until her manuscript found a home. Today, she's one of the most successful authors in the world.

Oprah Winfrey, despite a difficult childhood and numerous setbacks, overcame her limiting beliefs and fears. She transformed her life, becoming a media mogul, philanthropist, and advocate for self-improvement.

In conclusion, overcoming limiting beliefs and fears is a transformative process that paves the way for realizing your dreams. Recognize these mental barriers, challenge them, and act. As you do, you'll discover that the chains that once held you back can be broken, and your true potential can shine through, propelling you closer to yourdreams.

"I can't change the direction of the wind, but I can adjust my sails to always reach my destination."

- Jimmy Dean

CHAPTER 7

CULTIVATING A SUCCESS MINDSET: THE POWER OF YOUR MENTAL LANDSCAPE

"Success is not final, failure is not fatal: It is the courageto continue that counts."

- Winston Churchill

Your mindset is the lens through which you view theworld, your dreams, and your potential. Cultivating a success mindset is a transformative step on your journey to manifesting your dreams using the Dream Positioning System (DPS). In this chapter, we will explore the characteristics of a success mindset and provide strategiesfor developing and nurturing it. In the grand tapestry of life, our mindset serves as the vibrant thread that weavesthrough every experience, every decision, and every outcome. It's the compass that directs our actions, the architect of our dreams, and the sculptor of our reality. Cultivating a success mindset isn't merely about positive thinking; it's a profound transformation of how we perceive and engage with the world around us.

A success mindset is the cornerstone of achievement, thefuel that propels us forward in the pursuit of our dreams.It's a mental disposition characterized by resilience, optimism, adaptability, and a profound belief in one's ability to overcome challenges and thrive. But why is mindset so crucial?

Imagine two individuals, both faced with a daunting challenge in their careers. One has a fixed mindset, believing that their abilities are static, while the other possesses a growth mindset, perceiving challenges as opportunities to learn and improve. The one with a growth mindset is more likely to embrace the challenge, put in the effort to develop new skills, and ultimately, succeed. A success mindset isn't innate; it's cultivated through experiences, learning, and conscious effort. It often emerges from a combination of factors:

1. Early Influences:

Our upbringing plays a significant role in shaping our mindset. Children exposed to encouragement, support, and a belief in their potential are more likely to develop agrowth-oriented mindset. Conversely, those subjected tocriticism and negativity may adopt a fixed mindset.

2. Life Experiences:

Adversity can be a powerful catalyst for a success mindset.Facing and overcoming challenges instills resilience and the belief that difficulties can be surmounted. Consider individuals who have overcome personal setbacks, such asfinancial hardship or health issues, to achieve remarkablesuccess.

3. Learning and Growth:

Continuous learning fosters a success mindset. People who actively seek knowledge, embrace new experiences, and view failures as valuable lessons are more likely to cultivate this mindset. The pursuit of knowledge opens doors to new opportunities and perspectives.

Many entrepreneurs face numerous setbacks before achieving success. Their journey often involves failed ventures, financial struggles, and rejection. Yet, those who persist with a growth mindset are more likely to build thriving businesses.

In the world of sports, athletes with a success mindset notonly possess physical prowess but also mental resilience. They endure rigorous training, face fierce competition, and often recover from injuries, all driven by their unwavering belief in their potential.

Scientists and inventors who make groundbreaking discoveries often encounter numerous obstacles. ThomasEdison's relentless pursuit of the light bulb and Albert Einstein's determination to unlock the secrets of the universe exemplify how a success mindset can lead to transformative achievements.

Your mindset encompasses your beliefs, attitudes, and perceptions. It shapes your thoughts, emotions, and actions. It is a fundamental factor that influences your approach to challenges, your resilience in the face of setbacks, and your capacity to achieve your dreams.

Fixed vs. Growth Mindset

Psychologist Carol Dweck introduced the concept of fixed and growth mindsets. Understanding these mindsets can shed light on how individuals perceive their abilities and potential.

- **Fixed Mindset:** Individuals with a fixed mindset believe that their abilities and intelligence are static traits. They may avoid challenges to protect their self-esteem, give up easily, and view effort as fruitless. Failures are seen as reflections of their limitations.

- **Growth Mindset:** In contrast, those with a growth mindset believe that their abilities can be developed through dedication and hard work. They embrace challenges, persevere through setbacks, and see effort as a path to mastery. Failures are viewed as opportunities to learn and grow.

Cultivating a success mindset is not without its challenges. One common mindset obstacle is imposter syndrome, which is the feeling of being a fraud, despite evidence of your competence. To overcome this, you need to remind yourself of your accomplishments and expertise. Keep a record of your achievements to reinforce your self-belief. The fear of failure can paralyze you and prevent you from acting. To combat this requires focus on the process rather than the outcome. Embrace the idea that failures are steppingstones to success, not reflections of your worth. Comparing yourself to others can undermine your self-esteem. Instead, focus on your own progress and growth. Celebrate your unique journey and accomplishments. Self-doubt can creep in, especially when facing significant challenges. Combat it by keeping a journal of your successes and positive feedback. Surround yourself with a supportive network that boosts your confidence.

A success mindset comprises several essential components, designed to empower you and commit to your success. Believe in yourself and your abilities is at the core of a success mindset. Recognize your worth and your potential to achieve your dreams. A success mindset starts with a fundamental belief in the possibility of success. You have faith that your dreams are attainable and that your efforts can lead to positive outcomes. Being resilient is the ability to bounce back from setbacks and adversity. It's a hallmark of a success mindset. Rather than giving in to despair when faced with challenges, you view them as temporary obstacles on your path to success. A success mindset thrives on continuous growth and development. Seek knowledge, embrace new skills, and welcome change as a path to improvement. Maintain a positive attitude even in the face of adversity. Positivity fuels perseverance and helps you see opportunities where others see obstacles. Clearly defined goals provide direction and purpose. Know what you want to achieve and set specific, measurable, and achievable objectives. A proactive approach involves taking initiative and responsibility for your actions. Avoid a victim mentality and focus on what you can control. Individuals with a success mindset welcome challenges as opportunities for growth and learning. They see challenges not as threats but as steppingstones toward their goals. Passion fuels the pursuit of dreams. A success mindset is characterized by unwavering commitment and enthusiasm for your goals, which sustains your motivation over the long haul. Your internal dialogue plays a crucial role in your mindset.

Cultivate a habit of positive self-talk, where you challenge negative thoughts and replace them with affirmations that boost your self-confidence. A success mindset involves a thirst for knowledge and a willingness to learn from experiences, whether they are successes or failures. You continuously seek opportunities for self-improvement. Visualization is a powerful tool in cultivating a success mindset. Regularly visualize your success with clarity and emotion, reinforcing your belief in your ability to achieve your dreams. A success mindset is adaptable and flexible. It recognizes that change is inevitable and that the ability to adapt is a strength. It's about embracing change as a catalyst for growth.

Cultivating a success mindset is an ongoing process that requires dedication and self-awareness. Some strategies to help you develop and nurture this empowering mindset, is to Identify and confront limiting beliefs that hold you back. Replace them with empowering beliefs that align with your dreams and potential. Establish clear, specific goals that are aligned with your dreams. Setting and achieving these goals reinforces your belief in your abilities. Surround yourself with positive influences, including supportive friends, mentors, and motivational resources. Limit exposure to negativity and pessimism. Reframe your perspective on failure. See it as a valuable teacher rather than a reflection of your inadequacy. Embrace failures as opportunities to learn and grow. Cultivate a hunger for knowledge and self-improvement. Invest in your personal and professional growth through reading, courses, and skill development. Regularly practice visualization to reinforce your belief in success. Use positive affirmations to challenge and replace negative self-talk. A success mindset involves a willingnessto step out of your comfort zone and take calculated risks.These risks can lead to new opportunities and personal growth. Acknowledge and celebrate your achievements, no matter how small. Celebrations boost your self-esteem and motivate you to keep moving forward.

To cultivate a success mindset, pay attention to your inner dialogue. Replace self-doubt and negativity with affirmations that reinforce your self-belief. Commit tolifelong learning. Read books, attend seminars, and seek mentors who can expand your knowledge and skills. Embrace challenges as opportunities for growth. Developa resilience toolkit that includes strategies for coping with setbacks. Use the power of visualization to see yourself achieving your dreams. Visualizing success enhances motivation and focus. Associate with people who uplift and inspire you. Build a network of support and encouragement. Don't shy away from calculated risks.Assess the potential rewards and act when the opportunity aligns with your goals. Persistence is a hallmark of a success mindset. Keep pushing forward,even when faced with challenges or setbacks.

In our journey toward manifesting our Dream PositioningSystem (DPS), we must recognize the immense influence that words hold.

Words have power—power to shape our thoughts, our actions, and ultimately our reality. They are not mere expressions; they are the building blocks of our dreams and aspirations. Words are the bridge between intention and manifestation.

The first step in harnessing the power of words is to be mindful of the language we use. How often have youcaught yourself saying, "I hope," when talking about yourdreams? The word "hope" can be a double-edged sword. While it implies desire, it also leaves room for doubt. Instead of saying, "I hope to achieve my dreams," shift your language to, "When I achieve my dreams." This subtle change in wording conveys a sense of certainty and determination, setting the stage for success.

Another word we must be cautious of is "try." When we say, "I'll try to do this," we're creating an escape route for ourselves. Trying implies the possibility of failure without consequences. It allows us to avoid committing fully to our goals. Instead, replace "try" with "I will." By stating, "I will accomplish this," you instill a sense of commitment and responsibility in your endeavors. "I will" leaves no room for doubt; it asserts your determination to succeed.

It's crucial to understand that the universe listens to our words. When you say, "I can't afford this," you are, in that moment, closing the door to possibilities. The universe responds to your beliefs and intentions. If you've already decided that something is beyond your reach, the universe has no reason to work in your favor. Instead, adopt the mindset that everything is possible, and it's merely a matter of resourcefulness. Believe that you have the capability to access the resources necessary to achieve your dreams.

Let's also address the word "if." When you say, "What if this doesn't work?" or "What if I fail?" you're channeling your energy into scenarios that are out of your control. Focusing on "what ifs" leads to doubt, stagnation, and uncertainty, ultimately paving the way for quitting and failure. Instead, direct your energy toward what you truly want. Shift from "What if?" to "I am making this happen." Declare your intentions with confidence and conviction.

Words are not mere sounds; they are the architects of our reality. The way we speak to ourselves and to the universe can either empower our vision or hinder our progress. Choose your words wisely, for they hold the key to unlocking your dreams. As we continue our journey to manifest our DPS, let us remember that our words are thetools of creation, and through them, we shape our destiny.

Cultivating a success mindset is a lifelong endeavor that requires commitment and self-awareness. It is not a destination but a continuous journey of self-discovery andgrowth. By adopting the characteristics of a success mindset and implementing strategies to overcome mindset challenges, you empower yourself to pursue and achieve your dreams with unwavering belief and determination. Remember that success begins in the mind, and with the right mindset, you can overcome any obstacle on your path to greatness.

It is a success mindset is not just about achieving materialwealth; it's about embracing a way of thinking and being that empowers you to manifest your dreams. Remember the wisdom of Jonathan Becker and other thought leaders: Your beliefs and attitudes are the primary determinants of your success. By nurturing a success mindset, you unlock your potential to realize your aspirations and live a fulfilling life through the Dream Positioning System (DPS).

"Your attitude, not your aptitude, will determineyour altitude."
-Zig Ziglar

CHAPTER 8

TAKING INSPIRED ACTION: THE CRUCIAL CATALYST FOR SUCCESS

"When your determination changes everything else begin moving in the direction you desire.
The moment you resolve to be victorious - every nerve and fiber in your being immediately orients itself toward your success.
On the other hand - If you think "this is never going to work out" - that instant every cell in your being will bedeflated and give up the fight!
Then everything will move in the directionof failure!!!"

- Daisaku Ikeda

In your journey to manifest your dreams using the Dream Positioning System (DPS), one crucial step separates dreamers from achievers: taking inspired action. While a success mindset and clear goals are essential, they remaininert without action. In this chapter, we will explore the art of taking inspired action, which transforms your dreams from aspirations into tangible reality. Success is often perceived as a distant summit, a place where dreams come to fruition and aspirations are achieved. Yet, the path to this summit is not traversed by idle wishes alone; it is paved with deliberate, inspired action. Taking inspired action is the driving force that transforms mere desires into tangible results. In this exploration, we'll delve into why taking inspired action is not just important but critical for success. In the pursuit of your dreams, action isthe key that unlocks the door to success. It transforms your dreams from mere possibilities into tangible realities.By cultivating inspired action, setting meaningful goals, and embracing the journey with courage and determination, you can move steadily toward the realization of your most cherished dreams. Remember that every step you take brings you closer to the life you envision, and every action is a testament to your commitment to living your dreams to the fullest.

The Power of Action

Inspired action is the vibrant pulse of achievement. It's thedecision to step beyond the boundaries of comfort and into the realm of possibility. While dreams provide the destination, inspired action charts the course. It bridges the gap between the "what if" and the "what is."

Action is the bridge that connects your dreams to the physical world. It transforms your thoughts, beliefs, and intentions into concrete results. Without action, dreams remain ethereal, forever out of reach. Understanding thesignificance of action is the first step toward taking inspired steps toward your dreams.

Individuals who do not take inspired action may find themselves stuck in the same circumstances, yearning for change but unable to initiate it. This stagnation can lead to frustration and a sense of unfulfillment.

Inaction often translates to missed opportunities. Whether in career advancement, personal development, or relationships, failing to act can result in the loss of chances for growth and fulfillment.

Regret is a heavy burden to bear. Individuals who do not take inspired action often look back on their lives with a sense of missed potential. They wonder what could have been if they had acted upon their aspirations.

Strategies for taking inspired action begins by defining your goals clearly. When you have a clear target, it becomes easier to identify the actions required to reach it. Divide your goals into smaller, actionable steps. This makes them less overwhelming and more manageable. Visualization can be a powerful motivator. Imagineyourself achieving your goals and immerse yourself in the emotions associated with that success. Believe in your capabilities. Self-doubt can be a significant obstacle to acting. Surround yourself with supportive influences, as Daisaku Ikeda suggests, "Surround yourself with capable and outstanding individuals." Fear is a natural part oftaking risks. Acknowledge it, but don't let it paralyze you. As Les Brown aptly put it, "Too many of us are not living our dreams because we are living our fears." Consistency is key. Regular, deliberate steps, no matter how small, build momentum and create lasting change.

Action is not a monolithic concept. It spans a spectrum, ranging from small, daily steps to bold, transformative leaps. Depending on your goals and circumstances, different types of actions may be required. Incremental actions are small, manageable steps that move you closerto your goals. They are ideal for breaking down larger objectives into manageable pieces. For example, if your dream is to write a book, an incremental action could be writing 500 words each day. Strategic actions are deliberate and planned steps designed to achieve specificmilestones. They often require careful planning and execution. In the context of business, a strategic action might involve launching a new product or marketing campaign. Courageous actions are bold, transformative leaps that take you out of your comfort zone. They often involve risk and uncertainty but can lead to significant breakthroughs. Starting a new business, quitting a securejob to pursue a passion, or seeking a major life change areexamples of courageous actions. Consistent actions are those that you perform regularly and systematically. They build habits and routines that support your goals.Consistency is key to long-term success, whether in fitness, learning, or personal development.

Action turns your ideas and concepts into tangible products, services, or experiences. It is the mechanism through which you bring your dreams to life. Turning ideasinto reality is the alchemy of innovation and determination. It's the moment when inspiration takes form, where the abstract becomes concrete. This process is not just about wishful thinking; it's about the deliberate steps, unwavering belief, and relentless effort that transform a vision into a tangible achievement. Whether it's inventors bringing groundbreaking technologies to life, artists translating their imagination onto canvas, or entrepreneurs launching innovative businesses, turning ideas into reality is the testament to human potential and the driving force behind progress.

Acting breaks, the inertia of complacency and procrastination. It propels you out of your comfort zone and into the realm of progress and growth. Overcoming inertia is akin to breaking free from the gravitational pull of complacency and inaction. It signifies the conscious effort to propel oneself into motion, to surmount theresistance that often accompanies the status quo. Inertia,in both the physical and metaphorical sense, represents a state of rest or immobility. Overcoming it means summoning the energy and determination to initiate change, to step out of one's comfort zone, and to ventureinto the unknown. It is a vital catalyst for personal growthand progress, where the first step is often the most challenging, but also the most transformative.

Action is an invaluable teacher. It provides feedback, insights, and valuable lessons that help you refine your approach and make informed decisions. Learning throughexperience is the process by which knowledge is not only acquired but also internalized through hands-on involvement. It's a dynamic form of learning that goes beyond theoretical understanding and becomes deeply ingrained in one's memory and wisdom. An excellent example of this concept can be found in the journey of a novice chef who, despite reading countless cookbooks, truly comprehends the art of cooking only when they step into the kitchen, experiment with ingredients, make mistakes, and discover the nuances of flavor through trialand error. Through this direct experience, they gain a profound understanding of culinary techniques thattextbooks alone could never provide, illustrating the transformative power of learning by doing.

Each action you take builds momentum. Success breeds more success, and small actions can lead to significant achievements over time. Building momentum is like setting a wheel in motion; it requires initial effort, but once it's rolling, it becomes easier to keep it going. Momentum is a force that propels us toward our goals, creating a sense of energy and progress. Maintaining it is crucial because, much like a snowball rolling downhill, it grows larger and more powerful as it goes. In the pursuit of our dreams and ambitions, momentum is the wind at our back, pushing us forward even when challenges arise. It helps us stay focused, motivated, and resilient. To disrupt momentum often means expending extra effort torestart the process, while maintaining it ensures a smoother and more efficient journey toward our desired destination.

Taking inspired action involves aligning your actions with your dreams, passions, and purpose. It is about moving forward with enthusiasm and purpose, driven by your inner motivations. Before taking any action, clarify why you are pursuing a particular goal. Your "why" is the source of your motivation and passion. It connects your actions to your deeper values and aspirations. Clarifying your "why" is a pivotal aspect of cultivating inspired action because it provides a strong foundation and a powerful source of motivation. Your "why" represents the deeper purpose and meaning behind your actions, the driving force that fuels your determination even when faced withchallenges or setbacks. To arrive at a place where you willindeed take inspired action, it's essential to question your"why" on a profound level. This involves delving deep intoyour core values, beliefs, and aspirations. Ask yourself notonly what you want to achieve but why it matters to you personally. What impact will your actions have on your lifeand the lives of others? What values and principles are youupholding by pursuing this path? The more deeply you question and understand your "why," the more intrinsic and enduring your motivation becomes. It creates a powerful emotional connection to your goals, making it less likely for external obstacles or distractions to deter you. When your "why" is clear and compelling, it becomesthe guiding star that consistently propels you toward taking inspired action, even when faced with adversity.

Ensure that your goals are personally meaningful andaligned with your dreams. Meaningful goals evoke a sense of purpose and excitement, making it easier to act. Settingmeaningful goals is of paramount importance when it comes to cultivating inspired action. Meaningful goalsserve as the compass that directs your actions towards a purposeful destination. Meaningful goals provide a clear sense of direction and purpose. They answer the questionof where you want to go and what you want to achieve. This clarity eliminates ambiguity and helps you stay focused on what truly matters. When your goals are meaningful to you, they ignite a fire of passion and motivation within. These goals tap into your deepest desires and values, making you more committed to takingaction to achieve them. Meaningful goals act as a source of resilience. When faced with obstacles or setbacks, the significance of your goals provides the strength topersevere and overcome challenges. Your commitment tothe goal helps you weather the storms along the way. Meaningful goals can be measured, allowing you to track your progress. This measurable feedback not only keeps you motivated but also helps you adjust your actions as needed to stay on course. Achieving meaningful goals brings a profound sense of fulfillment and satisfaction. It reinforces the belief that your actions are aligned with your values and aspirations, creating a positive feedback loop that encourages further inspired action. Meaningful goals often transcend personal benefits. They can inspire and impact others positively, creating a ripple effect of motivation and action in your community or beyond.

Setting meaningful goals is the catalyst that transforms your desires into actions. They provide purpose, motivation, and a sense of achievement that drives you to take inspired action, making progress toward the fulfillment of your dreams and aspirations.

Regularly visualize yourself succeeding in your endeavors. Visualization strengthens your belief in your ability to achieve your dreams, motivating you to act. Visualizing success is a powerful technique used to cultivate inspired action by mentally rehearsing and experiencing the achievement of your goals or dreams before they happen.

It involves creating vivid mental images and scenarios that depict your desired outcomes. Visualizing success provides clarity about your goals. It allows you to see, in detail, what achieving your goals looks and feels like. For example, if your goal is to start a successful business, you might visualize yourself receiving positive customer reviews, managing a thriving team, and enjoying financial stability. Visualization ignites motivation and determination. When you vividly imagine your success, it stirs your emotions and reinforces your commitment to acting. For instance, if you're an aspiring athlete, you might visualize standing on the winner's podium, hearing the national anthem, and feeling the pride and joy of your accomplishment. Visualizing success can help you anticipate and prepare for challenges. For instance, if you're working towards a promotion, you might visualize yourself confidently addressing a difficult situation with your team or boss, effectively navigating through potential obstacles. Visualizing success boosts self- confidence. It helps you believe in your abilities and convinces your mind that success is attainable. For instance, if you're preparing for a public speaking engagement, you might visualize yourself delivering a powerful and engaging presentation to an applauding audience. Visualization can reduce anxiety and stress by creating a sense of familiarity with future situations. If you have an important job interview, visualizing yourself answering questions confidently and impressively can alleviate nervousness. Visualization ensures your actions align with your goals. It reminds you of the "why" behind your actions and keeps you on the path towards your desired outcomes. Athletes often use visualization to enhance their performance. For example, a golfer may visualize the perfect swing before taking the actual shot, increasing the chances of success.

Visualizing success is a mental practice that harnesses the power of your imagination to enhance motivation, confidence, and goal attainment. It's a tool that helps bridge the gap between where you are and where you want to be by aligning your thoughts and actions with your aspirations.

Develop a clear and actionable plan or roadmap for achieving your goals. Break down your objectives into smaller, manageable steps, and outline the actions required for each. Creating a roadmap is instrumental in achieving success because it provides a structured and clear path to follow. A roadmap outlines the steps and milestones necessary to reach your goals. It offers clarity on what needs to be done, when, and in what sequence. This clarity minimizes confusion and ensures you stay focused on the most critical tasks. A roadmap keeps your actions aligned with your objectives. It ensures that every task and decision is connected to your ultimate goals, preventing distractions or detours that could hinder your progress. With a roadmap, you can plan and allocate resources efficiently. You can prioritize tasks, allocate time and budget effectively, and avoid wasting resources on unnecessary activities. Seeing your goals laid out on a roadmap can be highly motivating. It serves as a visual reminder of what you're working towards, boosting your enthusiasm and dedication. A roadmap allows you to track your progress. You can see how far you've come and what remains to be done, which provides a sense of accomplishment and motivates you to keep moving forward. While a roadmap provides structure, it also allows for adaptability. Life often throws unexpected challenges and opportunities. A well-designed roadmap includes contingencies and flexibility to adjust to changing circumstances while staying on course. Sharing your roadmap with others or regularly reviewing it yourself can hold you accountable for your actions. It creates a sense of responsibility to stick to the plan and make consistent progress. By carefully planning and anticipating potential roadblocks, a roadmap can help you identify and mitigate risks. This proactive approach minimizes the chances of setbacks derailing your journey. A roadmap helps you manage your time effectively by breaking down tasks into manageable chunks. This prevents overwhelm and ensures you allocate sufficient time to each aspect of your journey. Success often involves long-term goals. A roadmap encourages you to think beyond short-term gains and keeps your focus on the bigger picture.

Creating a roadmap is like charting a course before embarking on a journey. It ensures that you have a clear, well-thought-out plan to guide your actions and decisions. This strategic approach significantly increases the likelihood of success by minimizing uncertainties and maximizing efficiency.

Understand that acting often involves risk and uncertainty. Embrace these challenges as opportunities for growth and learning. Courageous actions can lead to profound breakthroughs. Embracing risk and uncertainty is indeed essential in the process of cultivating inspired action. Risk and uncertainty are often the breeding grounds for growth and innovation. They push you out ofyour comfort zone, encourage creative thinking, and challenge the status quo. When you embrace them, you open yourself up to new possibilities and breakthroughs. Dealing with risk and uncertainty builds resilience. It teaches you to adapt to changing circumstances, stay calm under pressure, and bounce back from setbacks. These skills are invaluable in achieving long-term success. Embracing risk and uncertainty provides valuable learningopportunities. Even in failure, there are lessons to be gleaned that can inform future actions and decisions. It's through these experiences that personal and professionalgrowth occurs. Fear of the unknown often holds people back from acting. Embracing risk and uncertainty helps you confront and conquer these fears, empowering you tomove forward boldly. In today's dynamic world, playing itsafe can lead to stagnation. Embracing risk and uncertainty can give you a competitive advantage by positioning you as an agile and innovative thinker who is unafraid to take calculated risks.

However, while embracing risk and uncertainty is crucial, it's equally important to attempt to manage them to a reasonable extent. Managing risk involves making calculated decisions based on thorough assessment and analysis. It ensures that you're not blindly leaping into theunknown but rather taking informed risks. Managing risk includes implementing strategies to mitigate potential negative outcomes. This can involve contingency planning, diversification, or taking gradual steps rather than diving headfirst. Managing risk helps you allocate your resources (time, money, energy) more efficiently. It prevents putting all your eggs in one basket and allows fora more balanced approach to pursuing your goals. Excessive or poorly managed risk can lead to burnout or unsustainable practices. By managing risk, you ensure thatyour actions are sustainable in the long term.

While embracing risk and uncertainty is essential for growth and innovation, managing them is about making wise, informed decisions that balance the potential for reward with the potential for negative consequences. It'sabout taking calculated risks and being prepared to adaptas you navigate the uncertain path to your goals.

Share your goals and progress with someone you trust, such as a friend, mentor, or coach. Accountabilityencourages consistency and commitment. Staying accountable means taking responsibility for your actions, decisions, and commitments. It involves holding yourself answerable to the goals and plans you've set for yourself. Staying accountable requires acknowledging that you are the architect of your actions and outcomes. You takeownership of your choices and recognize that they have consequences, both positive and negative. It involves honoring the commitments you've made to yourself and others. When you set goals or make promises, you followthrough on them with dedication and integrity.Accountability often includes being transparent about your progress and results. You are open and honest about where you stand in relation to your goals, allowing for feedback and adjustments. Staying accountable requires consistency in your actions. You don't waver or make excuses when faced with challenges or setbacks. Instead, you maintain your commitment to your objectives. You establish clear metrics and milestones to track your progress. This enables you to evaluate whether you're ontrack and make necessary course corrections along the way. Accountability often involves practicing self- discipline. You resist distractions, procrastination, and temptations that could derail your progress towards your goals. When you encounter setbacks or failures, staying accountable means learning from them rather than placing blame elsewhere. You view mistakes as opportunities for growth and improvement. Accountability includes seeking feedback from mentors, peers, or coaches. You're open to constructive criticism and use it to refine your approach and make necessary changes. You persevere even when the going gets tough. Staying accountable means pushing through challenges and not giving up on your goals or dreams. Ultimately, staying accountable is results-oriented. You prioritize achieving your desired outcomes and take the necessary steps to make them a reality. Staying accountable is a fundamental aspect of cultivating inspired action becauseit ensures that you remain true to your aspirations and actively work towards them. It's a commitment to your personal and professional growth and a recognition that your actions have a direct impact on the achievement of your goals.

Surround yourself with sources of inspiration. Read books,listen to motivational speakers, and engage with communities that uplift and motivate you to act. Seeking inspiration is a vital step in cultivating inspired action, as itserves as a catalyst for motivation and purpose. Books, tapes, cd, podcast and other multimedia platforms serve as a continuous source of inspiration and motivation for me. This has served to be one of my primary sources of connection and focus. While in the gym I listen to audiblebooks, while riding in my car, for which I call "Drive Time University." I listen to motivational books and tape recordings. Many find inspirations in the beauty and serenity of nature. A walk in the woods, watching a sunset,or listening to the sound of waves can evoke a sense of awe and connection to the world, sparking motivation to protect and appreciate it. Literature, both fiction and non-fiction, is a rich source of inspiration. Reading about the journeys and achievements of others, their struggles and triumphs, can ignite a desire to act and follow one's own path.

Interacting with mentors and role models who have achieved what you aspire to can be highly inspiring. Learning from their experiences and hearing their stories can fuel your determination to pursue your goals. Artisticexpressions, whether in visual arts, music, dance, or otherforms, have the power to move and inspire. Creativity often sparks inspiration, encouraging you to explore yourown creative potential. Exploring new places, cultures, and perspectives can be profoundly inspiring. Traveling exposes you to diverse experiences and broadens your horizons, prompting you to act on your dreams and aspirations. Engaging with a supportive community of like- minded individuals can be motivating. Sharing ideas, experiences, and aspirations with others creates a sense of belonging and purpose that fuels action. Sometimes, facing challenges or adversity can be a powerful source ofinspiration. Overcoming obstacles can strengthen your resolve and inspire you to take action to improve your circumstances. Taking time for introspection and self- reflection can lead to deep insights and inspiration. It allows you to connect with your inner desires and values,prompting action aligned with your authentic self. Celebrating your own achievements and milestones, no matter how small, can be motivating. Recognizing your progress inspires you to continue working towards your goals. Repeating positive affirmations or mantras can inspire action by fostering a positive mindset. Affirmationsreinforce your belief in your abilities and yourcommitment to your dreams. Clarifying your purpose and values in life can be profoundly inspiring. When you align your actions with what truly matters to you, you are morelikely to take inspired and meaningful action. Hearing thestories of others who have overcome adversity or achieved great things can inspire you to believe in the possibility of your own success. Witnessing or engaging inacts of kindness and compassion can inspire you to make a positive impact in the world, motivating you to acttowards a greater purpose. Seeking inspiration from various sources enriches your perspective, ignites your passions, and fuels your determination to act. Inspiration serves as a driving force, reminding you of the potential within you and the significance of pursuing your dreams and goals.

Cultivate a growth mindset that welcomes challenges and sees failures as steppingstones to success. A growth mindset fosters resilience and a willingness to act. Maintaining a growth mindset is essential in cultivating inspired action because it shapes your attitude towards challenges, failures, and personal development. With a growth mindset, you believe that abilities and intelligence can be developed through dedication and hard work. I always say, "Leaders are Readers" A growth mindset encourages resilience in the face of setbacks. When you view failures as opportunities for growth rather than as fixed limitations, you're more likely to bounce back from adversity and maintain your motivation to pursue your goals. Those with a growth mindset embrace challenges as a chance to learn and improve. Instead of avoiding difficult tasks, they see them as opportunities to stretch their abilities and take inspired action. This mindset fosters a love for learning and personal development. It encourages you to seek new knowledge and skills, which can be instrumental in achieving your dreams and aspirations. People with a growth mindset understandthat effort and persistence are key to success. They are more willing to put in the hard work required to achieve their goals, knowing that progress is possible through dedication. Maintaining a growth mindset cultivatesoptimism. You believe that, with effort and learning, you can overcome obstacles and achieve your dreams, which fuels your motivation to take inspired action. In a constantly changing world, adaptability is crucial. A growth mindset encourages adaptability and the ability toembrace change as an opportunity for growth rather than a threat. This mindset promotes a healthy sense of self- esteem.

Instead of tying your self-worth to innate abilities, you value your efforts and progress, leading to greater confidence and a willingness to act. Ultimately, a growth mindset contributes to long-term success. It encourages you to persevere in the pursuit of your dreams and to view challenges as stepping stones rather than roadblocks. Maintaining a growth mindset is paramount in cultivating inspired action because it shapes your perspective and attitude towards your own potential and the challenges you encounter. It fosters resilience, adaptability, and a love for learning—all of which are critical for taking meaningful and sustained action toward your goals and dreams.

Procrastination is a common obstacle that can hinder inspired action. It is the tendency to delay or avoid tasks that need to be accomplished. To overcome procrastination, you must Identify your most important tasks and prioritize them. Focus on high-impact actions that align with your goals and dreams. Divide large tasks into smaller, more manageable steps. This reduces the sense of overwhelm and makes it easier to get started. Create a daily or weekly routine that includes dedicated time for acting on your goals. Consistency helps combat procrastination. If a task can be completed in two minutes or less, do it immediately. This small win can boost your motivation and productivity. Identify and minimize distractions that pull you away from acting. This may involve turning off notifications, creating a clutter-free workspace, or setting specific time limits for tasks. Establish clear deadlines for your actions and goals. Deadlines create a sense of urgency and accountability. Identify the times of day when you are most productive and alert and schedule your most important actions during these periods. Be kind to yourself when you encounter procrastination. Acknowledge that it is a common challenge and focus on progress, not perfection.

From Delaware to Paradise: Embracing Dreams and Taking Inspired

Action

My wife and I had always nurtured a profound dream of living in the tropical paradise of Hawaii. It was a dream that had taken root early in our marriage, and we decided to celebrate our 10th wedding anniversary with aHawaiian Luau theme, even though we were still firmly planted in our Delaware home. Amidst the hula dances and leis, we boldly announced our intention to move to Hawaii. Little did we know that the journey to our dream would be a circuitous one, marked by delays andunforeseen lessons.

As the years rolled by, we found ourselves in a peculiar situation. Our dream of living in Hawaii remained an unfulfilled desire. We had allowed ourselves to be trappedin a waiting game, believing that all the stars had to align, that our "ends" had to meet. Ironically, it was this belief that was holding us back. The very word "ends" suggests that they don't converge.

It was a vacation in Hawaii that became the turning pointin our story. Gazing at the breathtaking scenery and feeling the warmth of the island, we had an epiphany. Werealized that we needed to take inspired action, to break free from the cycle of waiting for circumstances to be perfect. It dawned on us that "ends" not meeting was justa reminder that life rarely aligns neatly.

With newfound determination, we decided to make our dream a reality. We reached out to my mother, promisingher a life in Hawaii by our side. We contacted a moving company, enlisted a realtor to sell our Delaware home, and set a relocation date. No more waiting for the universe to orchestrate our dreams; we were seizing control of our destiny.

As our resolve solidified, the universe seemed to conspirein our favor. Within months of our decision, we found ourselves preparing for a life in paradise. There was one comical hiccup - as the movers packed up our belongings,they casually asked for our

Hawaii address. It was then that we realized we hadn't secured a place to live beyond our initial four-day resort reservation. Homeless but undeterred, we trusted that everything would fall into place.

With a newfound faith in the journey, we arrived in Hawaii. On the very day, we checked out of our temporary lodging, we moved into a spacious four-bedroom home, complete with a master bedroom on the first floor for mymother's convenience. By month's end, our household goods arrived, fitting perfectly into our new home withoutrequiring storage.

Our story exemplifies a simple equation:

Speaking Dreams Into Existence + Taking Inspired Action = Success

It's a testament to the power of pursuing your dreams with unwavering determination and trusting that, in the end, the universe will conspire to make them come true.

The Dream Positioning System (DPS) is the guiding compass on this transformative journey, helping us unlockthe potential of our dreams to craft a life of purpose and fulfillment. Remember,

"A Dream Delayed is Never a Dream Denied."

Considering the stories of Daisaku Ikeda, a visionary leader and philosopher who took inspired action to promote peace, education, and cultural exchange through the Soka Gakkai International (SGI) movement. His relentless commitment to dialogue and mutual understanding has influenced millions globally. Ikeda's life embodies the principle that dreams, when fueled by unwavering action,can reshape the world.

In the world of entrepreneurship, innovators like Steve Jobs epitomize the concept of inspired action. Apple Inc. wasn't built solely on brilliant ideas; it thrived because Jobs and his team took bold, inspired actions to bring theirvisions to life. Each product launch, each new design, wasa manifestation of their dedication to innovation.

In the grand symphony of life, taking inspired action is the crescendo, the moment when potential transforms into reality. It is the force that propels individuals beyondlimitations, defies the odds, and achieves greatness. The stories of those who have taken inspired action, like Daisaku Ikeda, Steve Jobs, and Nelson Mandela, serve as beacons of inspiration, reminding us that the summit of success is not an elusive dream but a tangible destination,reached one step at a time. As you reflect on your own journey, remember that action is not merely the means toan end; it is the very essence of progress and the cornerstone of a life truly lived.

"Do not wait; the time will never be 'just right.' Startwhere you stand, and work with whatever tools youmay have at your command, and better tools will befound as you go along."

-Napoleon Hill

CHAPTER 9

PERSISTENCE AND RESILIENCE ON YOUR JOURNEY

"The true measure of a person's worth is not in theirpast accomplishments but in their ability to rise andovercome obstacles."

-Daisaku Ikeda

The Power of Persistence

Persistence is the determination to keep moving forward in the face of obstacles and adversity. It is the unwaveringcommitment to your dreams that enables you to overcome challenges and setbacks. Without persistence, dreams remain fragile and easily shattered.Understanding the power of persistence is crucial for achieving your goals.

In the pursuit of our dreams, we often encounter resistance and obstacles that test our resolve. It's during these challenging moments that our ability to persist andbe resilient truly shines.

As we navigate this chapter on persistence and resilience, we discover the synergy between strategic thinking and resilience. Let's explore how John Maxwell's strategic thinking, Matthew McConaughey's greenlight philosophy, and Wayne Dyer's principles of thought alignment harmonize to empower us in cultivating persistence and resilience:

Overcoming Resistance is a natural response to change and challenge. It often manifests as self-doubt, fear, or procrastination. Persistence is the force that pushes through resistance, allowing you to act despite these obstacles.

Resistance is like a formidable adversary that stands between us and our dreams. It can manifest in various forms, such as self-doubt, external criticism, or unexpected setbacks. Yet, it's through the act of overcoming this resistance that we develop the strength to persist. Resistance, in a way, serves as a gauge of how much we truly desire our goals. When we push through resistance, we prove to ourselves that our dreams are worth the effort.

Navigating Setbacks is inevitable on any journey. They can be discouraging and demotivating. However, persistence enables you to view setbacks as temporary detours rather than permanent roadblocks.

In fact, setbacks can be powerful catalysts for success. They provide us with valuable lessons, helping us refine our approach and avoid similar pitfalls in the future. Navigating setbacks not only empowers us with resilience but also builds the wisdom needed to make informed decisions on our path to success.

Consistency in action is like the steady beating of a drum, setting the rhythm for our journey. It's the daily commitment to taking small steps toward our goals that accumulates over time, creating significant progress. Consistency breeds discipline, and discipline is the bridge between our dreams and reality. When we show up consistently, we demonstrate our dedication to our aspirations, and this dedication is often rewarded with incremental but sustainable success.

Persistence ensures that you consistently act toward your goals. It prevents you from giving up prematurely and reminds you of your commitment to your dreams.

Many dreams require time and effort to master. Persistence is what keeps you learning, growing, and honing your skills until you reach a level of mastery.

Mastery of skills and objectives is the ultimate manifestation of persistence and resilience. It's the point where we not only achieve our dreams but also surpass them. Mastery comes through a relentless pursuit of improvement and a commitment to lifelong learning. It's the embodiment of consistent action, a willingness tolearn from setbacks, and an unwavering belief in one's ability to overcome challenges.

Resilience is the ability to bounce back from adversity and setbacks. It is the capacity to withstand challenges and continue your path, undeterred by difficulties. Resilience complements persistence and is essential for maintainingyour well-being and enthusiasm on your journey.

It enables you to adapt to change with grace and flexibility. It allows you to see change as an opportunity for growth rather than a threat.

Fostering emotional strength helps you manage stress, anxiety, and self-doubt. It equips you with copingmechanisms to navigate the emotional ups and downs ofpursuing your dreams.

Resilience encourages a growth mindset, where setbacks are seen as valuable learning experiences. It prevents setbacks from eroding your self-confidence and determination and helps you maintain perspective duringchallenging times. It allows you to see the bigger picture and understand that setbacks are temporary in the grandscheme of your journey.

Strategies for Cultivating Persistence and Resilience

Cultivating and strengthening persistence is a continuousprocess that involves mindset, motivation, and action.Strategies to help you harness the power of persistence on your journey would be to Revisit and reinforce your reasons for pursuing your dreams. Your "why" is the driving force behind your persistence. When your why is compelling and deeply meaningful, it fuels your determination. Set clear, specific goals provide a roadmapfor your persistence. Break your dreams into achievable milestones and set deadlines for each. This makes your journey more manageable and progress easier to measure. Having grit is a combination of passion andperseverance. It's the ability to stay committed to your long-term goals despite setbacks. Cultivate grit by consistently working on your dreams, even when motivation wanes. Your personal determination will insistthat you act. You must have and maintain a growth mindset. This embraces challenges and views failures as opportunities to learn and grow. Challenge your fixedbeliefs and embrace the idea that effort leads to improvement. Instead of dwelling on failures, focus on the lessons they offer. Analyze what went wrong, adjust your approach, and apply what you've learned to future actions.

An accountability partner makes a Hugh difference in one's success. Sharing your goals and progress with someone you trust—a friend, mentor, or coach. Accountability keeps you on track and provides external motivation. Additionally, it announces your goals, dreamsand desires to the universe for support and wisdom. Seeking guidance from individuals who have achieved similar dreams or faced similar challenges. Their experiences can provide valuable insights and motivation.

Resilience is a quality that can be nurtured and strengthened. It equips you to face adversity with grace and adaptability. A few strategies that will help you cultivate and harness resilience throughout your journey are, to treat yourself with kindness and understanding, especially during challenging times. Avoid self-criticism and negative self-talk, which can erode resilience. Enhance your ability to navigate challenges by developing problem-solving skills. Identify the specific issues you face and brainstorm potential solutions. Surround yourself with a supportive network of friends, family, mentors, andpeers. They can provide emotional support, guidance, and a sense of belonging. Mindfulness techniques, such as meditation and deep breathing, can help reduce stress and increase emotional resilience. They enable you to stay present and focused, even during difficult moments. Mindfulness and meditation are more crucial than you may think. By not creating space for this in your daily practice can be the single most important key holding you back from your objectives. Do not take this lightly!

Embrace change as a natural part of your journey. Cultivate adaptability by remaining open to new perspectives and flexible in your approach. Optimism is a powerful tool for resilience. Practice positive thinking and maintain a hopeful outlook, even in the face of challenges. Maintain realistic expectations about your journey. Understand that setbacks are normal, and that progress may not always be linear. "A Dream Delayed is not a Dream Denied."

Persistence and resilience are not separate qualities but intertwined forces that fortify your journey. They complement each other in a dance of determination and adaptability. As you persist in the pursuit of your dreams, resilience enables you to weather the storms and stay the course. Persistence comes into play when you face tasks that require ongoing effort and consistency. It drives you to take action, even when motivation is low, or progress is slow. Persistence keeps you on track toward your long- term goals. Resilience shines during moments of challenge and adversity. It enables you to bounce back from setbacks, learn from failures, and adapt to changing circumstances. Resilience allows you to maintain your well-being and emotional balance throughout your journey.

Throughout history, individuals who have achieved remarkable dreams have demonstrated extraordinary levels of persistence and resilience. Let's draw inspiration from a few of these stories:

Thomas Edison, the inventor of the light bulb, is famous for his persistence. He conducted thousands of experiments before successfully creating a practical electric light. His unwavering commitment to his vision is a testament to the power of persistence.

Before becoming a bestselling author of the Harry Potter series, J.K. Rowling faced numerous rejections from publishers. Her resilience and determination to share her story with the world eventually led to her unprecedented success.

Nelson Mandela's life is a testament to the extraordinary power of persistence and resilience in the face of seemingly insurmountable challenges. His story is not just a lesson in leadership; it's a profound example of the human spirit's ability to overcome adversity.

Mandela's journey began as a young lawyer in apartheid-era South Africa, where racial segregation and discrimination were deeply entrenched in society. Despite the oppressive regime, Mandela dedicated himself to fighting for justice and equality. He joined the African National Congress (ANC) and became a vocal advocate for peaceful resistance.

However, the government's response was brutal. In 1961, the ANC adopted a more militant stance, and Mandela was among those who embraced the armed struggle to end apartheid. This led to his arrest and, in 1964, a life sentence for his involvement in planning sabotage against the apartheid regime.

For 27 long years, Mandela endured imprisonment, isolation, and harsh labor, all the while remaining steadfast in his commitment to his cause. His unwavering determination and resilience turned him into a symbol of hope and resistance, both within South Africa and on the international stage.

In 1990, after immense pressure and international

condemnation, the South African government released Mandela from prison. Instead of seeking revenge, Mandela pursued reconciliation and forgiveness, famously leading negotiations that resulted in the end of apartheid and the country's first democratic elections in 1994.

Mandela's journey from prisoner to president demonstrated his ability to persist through unimaginable hardships and his unwavering resilience in the face of injustice. He didn't just break free from physical confinement; he also broke the chains of hatred and vengeance, choosing a path of unity and healing.

Nelson Mandela's life story continues to inspire people worldwide, serving as a reminder that persistence and resilience can bring about profound change, even in the darkest of times. His legacy teaches us that, no matter theobstacles, our dreams and ideals are worth the struggle.

In the award-winning book "Greenlights" by Matthew McConaughey, he uses an analogy of visualizing yourself approaching challenges with the spirit of a greenlight— seeing every obstacle as a potential source of growth andwisdom. His principles remind us that persistence is not about avoiding difficulties but about embracing them as essential milestones on our journey.

Wayne Dyer's Book "Change Your Thoughts, Change YourLife" Wayne explores the timeless wisdom of the Tao Te Ching. Dyer's interpretation emphasizes the power of aligning our thoughts with the natural flow of life. He teaches us that by changing our thoughts, we can changeour reality. Picture yourself internalizing this principle— shifting your thoughts from adversity to resilience, from doubt to determination. Dyer's teachings guide us to cultivate a mindset that not only endures but thrives in the face of adversity.

John Maxwell's Book "How Successful People Think" invites us to become strategic thinkers, envisioning success and crafting solutions in the face of challenges. Visualize yourself strategically analyzing obstacles and setbacks, using them as steppingstones toward your dreams. Imagine the power of clarity and purpose as you think strategically about your path. Each thought becomes a beacon of resilience, illuminating your way forward and helping you navigate life's complexities.

"The greatest glory in living lies not in never falling, but in rising every time we fall."

-Nelson Mandela

CHAPTER 10

THE POWER OF MEANINGFULRELATIONSHIPS

"True happiness is not found in isolation; it is found inthe hearts of others."

-Daisaku Ikeda

Meaningful relationships encompass a range of connections, from mentors and collaborators to friends and supporters. Meaningful relationships provide a network of support that bolsters your confidence and motivation. When you face challenges or setbacks, the encouragement of trusted individuals can make all the difference. Your connections can offer valuable insights and expertise. Mentors can provide guidance based on their experiences, helping you navigate your journey more effectively. Collaborative relationships open doors to shared resources, such as skills, knowledge, and opportunities. Partnerships can amplify your efforts and lead to greater success. Having accountability partners who share similar goals can help you stay on track. Additionally, witnessing the achievements of others can inspire you to reach higher and strive for more. Meaningful relationships contribute to your emotionalwell-being. They provide a sense of belonging, reduce feelings of isolation, and offer outlets for sharing joys andchallenges. Your connections introduce you to diverse perspectives and experiences, broadening your horizons and enriching your understanding of the world.

Imagine your journey becoming a force for positive change, as you cultivate relationships that transcend individual goals and contribute to a greater sense of unity.a life where your network of friends and allies is vast, a testament to your capacity to build meaningful connections. As we consider cultivating various types of meaningful relationships. Mentors are experienced individuals who can provide guidance, wisdom, and mentorship tailored to your goals. Their insights and advice can be invaluable. Collaborative relationships involve individuals or organizations that share common interests or complementary skills. Working together can lead to mutually beneficial outcomes. Your personal network, including friends and family, can offer emotionalsupport and encouragement. Sharing your dreams with loved ones can deepen your sense of purpose. Accountability partners are individuals with similar goals who help keep you on track by providing motivation and holding you responsible for your actions. Networking within your field or industry can lead to career opportunities, connections, and access to valuable resources.

Building meaningful relationships is an ongoing process that requires effort, authenticity, and reciprocity. Authenticity is the foundation of meaningful relationships. Be yourself, share your dreams and vulnerabilities, and letyour true self shine through. Look for individuals who share your values and goals. Common ground forms a strong foundation for connection and collaboration. Express gratitude and appreciation for the support and contributions of others. Acknowledging their efforts strengthens the bond. Practice active listening by giving your full attention and showing empathy. This fostersdeeper connections and understanding. Relationships area two-way street. Be willing to offer support, guidance, or resources in return when the opportunity arises. Clear andopen communication is key to any relationship. Ensure your intentions and expectations are understood and encourage open dialogue. Recognize that building meaningful relationships takes time. Be patient and understanding of others' schedules and commitments.

Reciprocity is the practice of giving and receiving in a balanced and mutually beneficial way. In meaningful relationships, reciprocity plays a significant role. It offers your support, advice, and assistance without expecting immediate returns. Be generous with your time and resources. When others offer their support or guidance, receive it graciously. Allow yourself to be helped, recognizing that reciprocity can take different forms. Reciprocity doesn't always occur in a linear or immediate fashion. It's about building trust and goodwill over time, where support flows back and forth. While reciprocity is important, it's essential to maintain healthy boundaries. Be mindful of not overextending yourself or feeling obligated to give more than you can. Mentorship is a powerful form of a meaningful relationship that can accelerate your journey.

When seeking mentors or becoming one yourself, keep inmind, to look for individuals who inspire you and possess the knowledge or experience you seek. Approach potential mentors respectfully and with a clear understanding of what you hope to gain from mentorship.It is a two-way exchange. Be open to learning from your mentor, and actively apply their advice and guidance. As you progress on your journey, consider mentoring otherswho may benefit from your experiences. Passing on your knowledge and support is a meaningful way to give back. Trust and respect are the cornerstones of mentorship. Build a relationship based on these principles, where bothparties feel safe and valued. Establish clear expectations and boundaries in your mentorship relationships. Discussgoals, frequency of interactions, and the desired outcomes.

Building and maintaining meaningful relationships can sometimes be challenging. Balancing relationships with your busy life can be difficult. Prioritize relationships that align with your goals and values and communicate openlyabout your availability. Conflicts may arise in any relationship. Address them directly and constructively, seeking resolution through open dialogue and compromise. As your journey progresses, circumstances and priorities may change. Communicate these changes with your relationships to maintain transparency. Overextending yourself in relationships can lead to burnout. Maintain boundaries and practice self-care to prevent exhaustion.

In Dale Carnegie's timeless book "How to Win Friends and Influence People", he delves into the art of building genuine connections with others. Carnegie's principlesrevolve around the power of empathy, active listening, and showing appreciation. He teaches us that success is not just about what we achieve but also about the qualityof our relationships. Imagine a life where every interactionis an opportunity to connect on a deeper level. Picture yourself as a Master of Communication and rapport- building, where people are drawn to you for your ability to make them feel heard, valued, and understood.

The Art of Connection and The Wisdom of Interconnectedness

To master the art of connection you must envision yourself as a skilled communicator, able to empathizewith others and make them feel valued. Picture relationships are flourishing because of your ability to genuinely connect with people.

Daisaku Ikeda's teachings on interconnectedness remind us of the profound impact our relationships can have on the world. Visualize a life where your interactions with others are rooted in empathy and compassion, fostering unity and understanding. Picture yourself as a bridge- builder, connecting people from diverse backgrounds and perspectives. Understanding and embracing this principlewill empower you to build meaningful relationships that align with your dreams and serve a higher purpose.

"The quality of your life is determined by the quality of your relationships."

-Tony Robbins

CHAPTER 11

WEALTH BUILDING STRATEGIES

"In today's fast-changing world, it's not so much what you know anymore that counts, because often what youknow is old. It's how fast you learn."

- Robert Kiyosaki

In manifesting your dreams using the Dream Positioning System (DPS), the concept of wealth extends beyond mere financial success. True wealth encompasses financial prosperity, personal fulfillment, and the ability to lead a purpose-driven life.

This chapter explores wealth-building strategies that encompass financial well-being, mindful spending, and the alignment of wealth with your dreams and values. Before diving into wealth-building strategies, it's essentialto redefine what wealth means to you personally. While financial abundance is a critical aspect, true wealth includes financial security and the ability to achieve your dreams without constant financial stress, which are integral to wealth. Wealth is not only about accumulating assets but also about deriving joy, satisfaction, and purpose from your endeavors. Good health is a form of wealth. Prioritizing your physical and mental well-being ensures that you can enjoy your prosperity. Meaningful relationships, connections, and a supportive community contribute significantly to your overall wealth. Wealthgrants you the freedom to make choices aligned with yourvalues and passions, leading to a more fulfilling life.

Redefining Wealth

Wealth building begins with mindful financial management. This includes strategies to earn, save, invest, and grow your financial resources. Therefore, you must define your financial objectives, whether it's saving for a home, starting a business, or achieving financial independence. Clear goals provide direction. Create a budget that aligns with your goals and values. Track your income and expenses to ensure you're living within your means. Establish a savings plan and automate your savings. Consider different investment vehicles, such as stocks, bonds, real estate, and retirement accounts, to grow your wealth over time. Diversification helps mitigate risk in your investment portfolio. Spread your investments across various asset classes to minimize potential losses. Continuously educate yourself about personal finance, investments, and wealth-building strategies. Knowledge is a powerful tool for managing your finances effectively. Prioritize paying off high-interest debts, such as credit card debt, while strategically managing lower-interest debts, such as mortgages or student loans. Consider working with financial advisors or planners who can provide personalized advice based on your financial goals and circumstances.

Establish venues that creates passive income. Passive income streams play a vital role in wealth building. Passive income refers to money earned with minimal effort on your part once the initial setup is complete. Dividend- paying stocks, rental properties, and interest from bonds or savings accounts are examples of investment-based passive income. If you have intellectual property, such as books, music, or patents, you can earn royalties each time your work is used or sold. Owning and renting out properties can provide a consistent source of passive income. If you have a successful business, you can earn passive income by hiring managers to run the day-to-day operations. Online platforms allow you to lend money to individuals or businesses in exchange for interest payments. Diversifying your sources of passive income can provide financial stability and help you achieve your wealth-building goals more quickly.

Wealth becomes truly meaningful when it aligns with your dreams and values. Therefore, it's important to Identify your core values, such as family, philanthropy, environmental consciousness, or personal growth. Ensurethat your wealth-building strategies align with these values. Allocate time and resources to pursue your passions and interests. Wealth should enhance your ability to live a purpose-driven life. Incorporate charitable giving into your financial plan. Supporting causes thatresonate with your values can be a fulfilling aspect of wealth. Wealth building should not come at the cost of your physical and mental well-being or relationships. Strive for balance in all aspects of your life. Periodically assess your wealth-building journey to ensure it remains aligned with your dreams and values. Adjust your strategies as needed.

Building sustainable wealth requires a long-term perspective and disciplined strategies. Creating Multiple Income Streams will afford you the ability to diversify yourincome sources to reduce dependence on a single paycheck or business. This can include a combination of active and passive income. Consistently save and invest aportion of your income, even during times of financial abundance," Pay Yourself First.". Before paying any bills, pay yourself first, a good rule of thumb is to pay yourself 10 to 20% of your gross monthly income, every month. When you pay yourself first, you allocate a portion of your income to savings or investments before covering other expenses. This ensures that saving becomes a non- negotiable priority rather than an afterthought. By makingit a habit to save or invest a portion of your income first, you establish consistency in your financial planning. Regular contributions, even if they are small, can accumulate significantly over time. Paying yourself first helps you build an emergency fund. This fund acts as a financial safety net, providing you with resources to cover unexpected expenses without derailing your financial goals. Over time, the money you save or invest through this strategy can grow substantially due to compound interest. Compound interest allows your savings to earn interest on the interest earned previously, accelerating wealth accumulation. Prioritizing saving or investing before spending on discretionary items cultivates financial discipline. It encourages you to live within your means and make intentional choices about your expenses. Whether your financial goals involve buying a home, retiring comfortably, or achieving other milestones, paying yourself first ensures that you're actively working toward these objectives. Having a financial cushion from paying yourself first can reduce stress and anxiety associated with money. It provides peace of mind knowing that you're prepared for unexpected financial challenges. This strategy encourages a shift from a consumption-oriented mindset to an investment-oriented one. It reinforces the idea that your future financial security is as important as your current lifestyle. Ultimately, paying yourself first is a crucial step toward achieving financial independence. It empowers you to rely on your investments and savings rather than solely on earned income for financial support. Ultimately paying yourself first is a foundational wealth- building strategy because it establishes a strong financial foundation, promotes consistent savings, and aligns your financial habits with your long-term goals. It's a proactive approach to building wealth and securing your financial future.

Understand how compound interest can significantly grow your wealth over time. Stay informed about financial markets and trends. Be willing to adapt your investment strategies based on changing circumstances. Regularly review your investment portfolio to ensure it aligns with your goals and risk tolerance. Rebalance your assets when necessary. Consider strategies for wealth preservation, such as estate planning, insurance, and asset protection. Protecting your wealth is as important as building it. Understanding the value of Trust is also extremely important. There are various types of Trust, it's important for you to know what they do and evaluate how they mayalign with your strategy. Embarking on a journey of continuous financial education, expanding your knowledge of money management, investments, and wealth-building strategies.

Mindfulness, the practice of being fully present in the moment, can greatly enhance your wealth-building journey. Mindfulness helps you become more aware of your financial habits, including spending patterns and impulsive decisions. Mindfulness techniques, such as meditation, can reduce stress and anxiety related to financial matters, allowing you to make clearer decisions.Being present in the moment allows you to make more thoughtful and informed financial decisions. Mindfulness fosters a sense of gratitude for what you have, reducing the tendency to pursue wealth for its own sake.

As we explore the art of wealth building, we'll delve into principles and strategies for achieving financial success. Imagine yourself embarking on a journey of continuous financial education, expanding your knowledge of moneymanagement, investments, and wealth-building strategies. It is important for you to become financially literate. This will be enabling you to make informed decisions that lead to financial prosperity. Visualize your life filled with income-generating assets that work for you. Whether through real estate investments, stocks, or entrepreneurial ventures, picture yourself strategically accumulating assets that provide ongoing passive income and create long-term wealth. Picture the freedom that comes with multiple passive income streams. This will empower you to diversify your income sources, ensuring financial stability and reducing reliance on traditional employment. Envision yourself with a portfolio of income-producing assets that allow you to live life on your terms.Imagine becoming a shrewd investor who makes well- informed decisions in the world of finance. Picture yourself analyzing investment opportunities with confidence, strategically allocating resources to maximizereturns, and securing your financial future. Visualize yourlife filled with income-generating assets that work for you. Whether through real estate investments, stocks, or entrepreneurial ventures, picture yourself strategically accumulating assets that provide ongoing passive income and create long-term wealth. Create a portfolio of income-producing assets that allow you to live life on yourterms. Hill's teachings underscore the importance of persistence in the pursuit of your financial goals, ensuringthat you stay committed to creating and maintaining these income streams.

"An investment in knowledge pays the best interest."
- Benjamin Franklin

CHAPTER 12

LIVING A LIFE OF PURPOSEAND CONTRIBUTION

"The meaning of life is to find your gift. The purpose oflife is to give it away."

-Pablo Picasso

In the journey of manifesting your Dream Positioning System (DPS) and embracing a life of purpose and contribution, the concept of cultivating an abundancemindset plays a pivotal role in determining your success. It's essential to recognize that abundance extends farbeyond the confines of material wealth, encompassing allaspects of existence, including opportunities, relationships, and personal growth. Shifting from amindset of scarcity to one of abundance holds the potential to ignite profound transformations in our lives, empowering us to pursue our dreams with unwavering confidence.

Abundance as a Holistic Concept: Abundance, often narrowly associated with monetary riches, transcends this notion. It encompasses the richness of life experiences, the wealth of meaningful relationships, and the boundless opportunities for personal growth. Abundance is the belief in an abundance of resources, both seen and unseen, waiting to be tapped into.

Transformation through Mindset Shift: Shifting from a scarcity mindset to an abundance mindset transforms ourperception of the world. Instead of dwelling on limitations, we see boundless possibilities. This shift liberates us from the paralyzing fear of inadequacy and failure, empowering us to take courageous strides towardour dreams.

Practical Strategies for Embracing Abundance: Embracing abundance is not theoretical but practical. It necessitates a conscious decision to view life positively, to have faith in our potential, and to operate from a place of generosity. Real-life examples illuminate these practical strategies, offering readers a tangible roadmap to follow.

The Power of Giving: Integral to the abundance mindset is the act of giving. The chapter emphasizes that genuine giving is unconditional, flowing from the heart. It underscores the principle that when we give without expecting anything in return, we align with the natural flow of abundance.

The Current of Life: Drawing a metaphorical connection between "currency" and "current," this chapter illustratesthat, much like the ceaseless flow of the ocean's current, the current of our lives is perpetually in motion. Embracing abundance involves recognizing that life's currents offer opportunities and experiences aligned withour mindset.

The Servant Mindset: Living a life of abundance is synonymous with living a life of service. It accentuates giving from the heart, utilizing our talents and gifts to uplift others. It underscores that acts of service have a ripple effect, enriching both the giver and the receiver.

An African proverb poignantly encapsulates this essence:

"The hands that oil the feet are in return oiled by the feet."

By embodying an abundance mindset and choosing to bea giver rather than a taker, individuals can not only manifest their DPS but also embark on a transformative journey marked by personal growth, fulfillment, and an expansive abundance transcending mere material wealth.

The Power of Purpose: Purpose serves as the driving forceinfusing life with meaning and direction. It provides clarityabout goals and a profound connection to something larger than oneself. Purpose ignites motivation and fuels passion. With a clear sense of purpose, individuals are driven to act, overcome challenges, and persist in the pursuit of their dreams, even in adversity.

Fulfillment and Well-being: Living with purpose contributes significantly to overall well-being and deep fulfillment. It enables individuals to find joy and satisfaction in daily life, fostering a sense of contentment.

Creating Connections and Impact: Purpose extends beyond personal fulfillment; it propels individuals to make a positive impact on the world. It fosters connections withothers, creating a sense of community and belonging. Purpose often drives individuals to contribute to causes larger than themselves, channeling their energy toward the betterment of society.

Discovering Your Purpose: Discovering or clarifying your sense of purpose is a deeply personal journey. It can be guided by:

- **Core Values and Beliefs:** Identify the values and beliefs you hold dear and are willing to stand up for.

- **Passions and Fulfilling Activities:** Consider activities and interests that bring you profound joy and fulfillment.

- **Unique Strengths and Talents:** Recognize your individual strengths, talents, and skills.

- **Impact and Legacy:** Reflect on the impact you wish tohave on the world and the legacy you want to leave behind.

- **Inspiring Models:** Seek inspiration from individuals whose purposeful lives resonate with you.

Contributing to the World: Living a life of purpose and contribution often involves giving back to society or the community. You can contribute by:

- **Supporting Causes:** Find organizations or causes aligned with your values and offer your time, skills, orresources.

- **Financial Donations:** Consider donating to charitable organizations or causes close to your heart.

- **Mentorship:** Share your knowledge, experience, and expertise with others through mentorship.

- **Sustainability:** Promote sustainability and reduce your environmental impact.

- **Advocacy:** Use your voice to advocate for social justiceand positive change.

- **Creative Expression:** Leverage creative forms like art, writing, or music to inspire, educate, or uplift.

- **Acts of Kindness:** Simple acts of kindness can have aripple effect of positivity.

While living a life of purpose and contribution is fulfilling, maintaining balance is vital. Prioritize self-care, setboundaries, and manage your time effectively. Review your commitments periodically to ensure they align with your evolving sense of purpose.

A Personal Story: My daughter Shay's journey as an entrepreneur exemplifies finding purpose in one's work. She started a sustainable fashion brand due to her passionfor ethical and eco-friendly fashion. As her business grew,Shay realized she could do more than create stylish clothing; she could use her platform to advocate for sustainability in the fashion industry. Her purpose evolvedto include not just running a successful business but also contributing to positive change.

Inspirational Figures: Les Brown, Daisaku Ikeda, and Barack Obama offer valuable insights into living a life of purpose and contribution. Les Brown emphasizes finding your unique "why" to fuel your actions and inspire others.Daisaku Ikeda underscores the transformative power of faith in oneself and the importance of compassion. BarackObama highlights the significance of hope, unity, and collective action in creating positive change.

Remember, living a life of purpose and contribution is an ongoing journey. As you pursue your dreams with the DPS,recognize that true fulfillment comes not only from achieving personal goals but also from making a positive impact on the world. Your sense of purpose can guide you toward a life where your actions and contributions leave a lasting, positive imprint on others and the world itself.

"Service to others is the rent you pay for your room here on Earth."

- Muhammad Ali

CHAPTER 13

SPIRITUALITY AND ALIGNMENT WITHYOUR DREAMS

"The heart that seeks for happiness for others is notseparate from the heart that seeks happiness for oneself."

-Daisaku Ikeda

Spirituality, often defined as a sense of connection tosomething greater than us, plays a profound role in our lives. It can provide a sense of purpose, inner peace, and guidance on our journey to manifest our dreams using theDream Positioning System (DPS). The importance of spirituality and alignment with your dreams in manifesting your DPS (Dream Positioning System) cannot be understated. This principle taps into the deep connection between one's inner beliefs, values, and dreams, and it plays a pivotal role in shaping the course of one's life.

The Essence of Spirituality

Spirituality often leads to a clearer sense of purpose. When individuals align their spiritual beliefs with their dreams, they gain a deeper understanding of what truly matters to them. This clarity acts as a guiding light, directing their actions and decisions towards the fulfillment of their dreams. It can provide individuals withthe inner strength and resilience needed to overcome challenges and setbacks on their journey. It instills a senseof faith and trust in the process, even in the face ofadversity. When individuals align their dreams with their spiritual values, their actions become more authentic andaligned with their true selves. This authenticity resonateswith others and often attracts support and collaboration. Spirituality often involves practices of mindfulness and introspection. This heightened awareness allows individuals to recognize opportunities and make intuitive decisions that are in line with their dreams. Some believe that aligning with one's dreams at a spiritual level connects them to a larger universal consciousness. This resonance can lead to serendipitous events and opportunities that support the realization of their dreams.

Mahatma Gandhi is a classic example of someone whose spirituality was deeply aligned with his dream of Indian independence and social justice. His unwavering commitment to nonviolent resistance, rooted in his spiritual beliefs, led to significant political and social change.

Spirituality is a deeply personal and multifaceted concept. It encompasses beliefs, values, and experiences that transcend the material world. Many people find spirituality through their connection to a higher power, whether it's through religion, nature, or a sense of cosmic unity. Spirituality often involves introspection and self- discovery, seeking answers to life's fundamental questions and the nature of existence. It provides a framework for understanding our purpose in life and the significance of our actions. Spirituality can inspire acts of kindness, empathy, and service to others, reflecting a sense of interconnectedness. It offers a path to inner peace and resilience in the face of life's challenges.

The journey to manifest your dreams begins with self- mastery. It involves overcoming inner obstacles, doubts, and limitations. True victory lies in conquering your own doubts and fears. Challenges and setbacks are an integral part of any journey. They are opportunities for growth and self-discovery. Embrace adversity as a means of cultivating the determination to achieve your dreams. Altruism and the desire for personal success are not mutually exclusive.In fact, they are interconnected. Your pursuit of dreams can have a positive impact on others, and in helping themachieve happiness, you find your own fulfillment.

Aligning Spirituality with Your Dreams Begin by reflecting on your core values. What principles guide your life? Howdo these values align with your dreams? Ensure that yourgoals resonate with your deeply held beliefs. Ensure that your dreams are ethically sound and contribute positivelyto the world. Aligning your aspirations with ethical principles enhances your sense of purpose and fulfillment. Spiritual practices, such as meditation, prayer, or mindfulness, can cultivate inner peace and resilience. Thisinner calm can be a source of strength as you pursue yourdreams. Recognize and appreciate the blessings in your life. Gratitude fosters a positive outlook and a deeper sense of contentment, making your journey more meaningful. Spirituality often involves a sense of interconnectedness. Foster meaningful connections with others who share your dreams or values. Collaboration and support can propel you forward. Whether through religious leaders, mentors, or your own inner reflection, seek guidance and wisdom to navigate the complexities ofyour dreams. External guidance can shed light on your path. Spirituality can help you confront and overcome fear. It encourages you to embrace uncertainty with courage and faith in the journey ahead.

The Power of Visualization and Affirmation is throughmentally picturing your desired outcomes. By regularly visualizing your dreams, you reinforce your commitment and belief in their realization. Affirmations are positive statements that reinforce your beliefs and goals. Repeating affirmations daily can strengthen your resolve and maintain a positive mindset. Embracing a Holistic Approach creates alignment with your dreams andspirituality should be a holistic endeavor. It nourishes yourphysical and mental well-being. A healthy body and mind provide a strong foundation for pursuing your dreams. Prioritize self-care practices that promote balance, such as exercise, nutrition, sleep, and stress management. It Incorporate mindfulness practices into your daily routine. Mindfulness enhances self-awareness and helps you stay attuned to your sense of purpose, and it embraces changeand adaptability. Life's journey is dynamic, and your dreams may evolve. Being open to change ensures continued alignment with your purpose.

Nelson Mandela's 27-year imprisonment for his fight against apartheid in South Africa was marked by his unwavering inner strength. His alignment with the dreamof a racially unified and just nation was deeply rooted in his spiritual beliefs, which sustained him during difficult times.

In conclusion, spirituality and alignment with your dreams are integral components of the DPS (Dream Positioning System). They provide the foundation for clarity, resilience, authenticity, mindfulness, and a deep connection to the universe—all of which contribute to thesuccessful manifestation of one's dreams. The examples of individuals mentioned above demonstrate the transformative power of this principle in real-world scenarios, reinforcing its importance in the pursuit of a purposeful and fulfilling life. The fusion of faith, interfaithwisdom, and spirituality will empower you to live a life where your dreams are not just personal goals but also spiritual quests. Your journey becomes a sacred pilgrimage, guided by inner wisdom and a profound sense of purpose.

"Your spirituality is not separate from your daily life; it'swoven into every action and decision you make."

-Unknown

C H A P T E R 14

MANIFESTING ABUNDANCE IN HEALTHAND WELLNESS

"You must learn to get in touch with the innermost essence of your being. This true essence is beyond theego. It is fearless; it is free; it is immune to criticism; itdoes not fear any challenge. It is beneath no one, superior to no one, and full of magic, mystery, and enchantment.

-Deepak Chopra

Manifesting abundance in health and wellness is a vital component of the DPS Dream Positioning System because it recognizes that physical and mental well-being are the foundation upon which all other dreams and aspirations are built. When you are in good health and have a strong sense of wellness, you are better equipped to pursue yourgoals and make your dreams a reality. Good health provides you with the energy and vitality needed to take inspired action towards your dreams. When you'rephysically fit, you have the stamina to work hard, overcome obstacles, and persevere on your journey. Wellness isn't just about physical health; it also includes mental well-being. A clear and focused mind is essential for setting and achieving goals. Manifesting mental abundance means cultivating positive thoughts, managingstress, and developing resilience. Emotional health is another aspect of wellness. People who can navigate theiremotions effectively are better equipped to handle setbacks and maintain their persistence on the path to their dreams. Emotional abundance involves practices like mindfulness, self-awareness, and emotional intelligence. Achieving your dreams often requires a balanced life. Prioritizing health and wellness helps you strike that balance. It means making time for self-care, exercise, proper nutrition, and adequate rest. Your journey towardshealth and wellness can inspire others to do the same. When people see you manifesting abundance in this area,they may be motivated to follow suit, creating a ripple effect of well-being in your community. Good health increases your chances of a long and fulfilling life. This means more time to work towards your dreams and enjoythe fruits of your labor.

Manifesting abundance in health and wellness is about taking a holistic approach to your well-being. This includes not only physical fitness but also mental and emotional wellness. People like Deepak Chopra have dedicated theircareers to promoting holistic health practices that align with the DPS philosophy. He emphasizes a holistic approach to health—one that considers the interconnectedness of the mind, body, and spirit.

To manifest abundance in health and wellness, it's essential to adopt this holistic perspective. The principle of manifesting abundance in health and wellness into yourDPS journey ensures that you have the strength, clarity, and resilience needed to pursue your dreams with vigor and purpose. It's a reminder that your well-being is the foundation upon which your aspirations can thrive. Recognize the profound influence of your thoughts, emotions, and beliefs on your physical health. A positive mindset can promote well-being. Strive for balance in all aspects of life, including work, relationships, and leisure. A harmonious life contributes to overall health.Understand the importance of a healthy diet and proper nutrition. The food you consume has a direct impact on your vitality. Regular exercise and movement are essentialfor physical fitness and mental clarity. Find activities you enjoy staying active. Develop effective stress- management techniques, such as meditation, deep breathing, or mindfulness, to reduce the negative impact of stress on your health. Cultivate emotional intelligence and resilience. Emotions can significantly affect your physical health, so it's vital to address them constructively.Prioritize restorative sleep and relaxation. Quality rest is essential for physical and mental rejuvenation.

Your relationships and connections with others profoundly impact your emotional and physical health. Openness and compassion toward others contribute to overall wellness.

Longevity alone is not the goal; it's about living a life filledwith purpose, vitality, and joy. Health and wellness enableyou to make the most of your years. Begin by acknowledging how to approach your meals with mindfulness. Pay attention to what you eat, savor each bite, and choose nourishing foods that support your health goals. Create a fitness routine that suits your preferences and lifestyle. Consistent physical activity boosts your energy, strengthens your body, and enhances your mood. Incorporate stress-reduction practices into your daily routine. Meditation, yoga, or even a quiet moment of reflection can help you manage stress effectively. Prioritize sleep hygiene to ensure restful and rejuvenating sleep. Create a calming bedtime routine and maintain a consistent sleep schedule. Nurture your emotional well-being by practicing self-compassion, seeking support when needed, and expressing your feelings constructively. Regular health check-ups and preventive measures are essential for maintaining your well-being. Be proactive in monitoring your health.

The Role of Mind-Body Healing

Employ mind-body healing techniques. Meditation is a powerful tool for reducing stress, enhancing self- awareness, and promoting mental clarity. Regular meditation practices can improve overall well-being. Yoga combines physical postures, breath control, and meditation to promote flexibility, strength, and inner peace. It is an excellent practice for holistic well-being. Mindfulness practices involve paying deliberate attentionto the present moment. Mindfulness can reduce anxiety, enhance focus, and improve overall mental health.

Abundance in health extends beyond physical well-being to emotional and spiritual health. Treat yourself with the same kindness and compassion you offer to others. Self- compassion is essential for emotional health. Release theburden of grudges and resentments. Forgiveness is a gift you give yourself, freeing you from emotional baggage.

Embrace gratitude as a daily practice. Recognize and appreciate the blessings in your life, fostering a positive outlook. Engage in meaningful relationships and build a supportive community. Social connections are vital for emotional well-being. Explore your spirituality and beliefs. A sense of purpose and connection to something greater than yourself can enhance overall well-being.

Manifesting abundance in health and wellness is a lifelongjourney that intertwines with your pursuit of dreams. By adopting a holistic perspective, nurturing your mind, body, and spirit, and drawing inspiration from others wisdom, you can cultivate well-being and vitality thatsupport you on. Abundance Meditation is a transformative practice that centers on manifesting and attracting abundance in all aspects of life, including health and wellness. This practice involves aligning your thoughts, feelings, and intentions to draw positivity and abundance into your life. It emphasizes that abundance begins with a mindset of prosperity and well-being. Abundance Meditation invites you to imagine a life whereyour health radiates vitality, where wealth is not just financial but extends to the richness of your overall well- being, and where happiness flows naturally from your state of abundance. Picture yourself as someone whoeffortlessly attracts health, wealth, and happiness through the power of your intentions and meditationpractice.

The fusion of holistic health and abundance meditation will empower you to create a life where well-being is not just a goal but a foundational element of your dreams.

Your journey becomes a holistic quest for abundance, where health and vitality are integral components of yourpursuit.

"The power of intention is the power to manifest, tocreate, to live a life of unlimited abundance, and to attract into your life the right people at the right moments."

-Wayne Dyer

CHAPTER 15

CELEBRATING YOUR ACHIEVEMENTSAND SETTING NEW GOALS

"Each day is a chance to celebrate your existence and set new goals. Make the most of every opportunity, andyour life will be a continuous celebration."

- Daisaku Ikeda

Celebrating your achievements and setting new goals is acritical aspect of manifesting your DPS Dream PositioningSystem (DPS). This practice is a continuous cycle of growthand fulfillment that keeps you motivated, focused, and aligned with your dreams. Celebrating your achievements,whether big or small, provides a sense of accomplishmentand motivation. It's like a pat on your own back, remindingyou of your progress and keeping your momentum going. This motivation is essential for staying committed to your DPS journey. When you celebrate your achievements, youtake time to reflect on how far you've come. This reflection is crucial for maintaining a positive attitude anda sense of gratitude. It allows you to appreciate the journey and the effort you've invested. Setting and achieving goals builds your confidence. When you acknowledge your accomplishments, you reinforce thebelief that you can succeed. Confidence is a powerful toolfor overcoming obstacles and setbacks on your path to manifesting your dreams. After celebrating your achievements, it's essential to set new goals. This processkeeps you moving forward, preventing stagnation. Your DPS is not a static destination; it's a dynamic journey. By setting new goals, you create new challenges andopportunities for growth. Setting new goals allows you torealign with your dreams continually. As you achieve yourcurrent goals, your dreams may evolve or become clearer.By setting new objectives, you ensure that your actions are always aligned with your current aspirations. The DPSDream Positioning System recognizes that life is dynamic, and circumstances change. Celebrating achievements andsetting new goals is a way of adapting to these changes and remaining innovative. It's about staying relevant and flexible on your journey. Passion and purpose are the driving forces behind your DPS. Celebrating achievementsand setting new goals keeps these fires burning. It remindsyou why you embarked on this journey in the first place and rekindles your determination. This practice instills a sense of responsibility and accountability. When you celebrate your achievements and set new goals, you are acknowledging your role in creating your life. You become the author of your destiny, which is a fundamental principle of DPS. Your journey can inspire others. When people see you celebrating your achievements andcontinuously setting new goals, they may be motivated todo the same. Your example can have a positive impact on your family, friends, and community. Celebrating achievements and setting new goals ensures a holistic approach to fulfillment. It's not just about reaching milestones but about enjoying the entire journey. This holistic fulfillment is a cornerstone of DPS.

Embracing the Power of Gratitude

Celebrating your achievements is a vital step in recognizing your progress and finding fulfillment in your journey. Gratitude is a powerful tool for celebrating your achievements. Take time to reflect on and express gratitude for the progress you've made on your dream journey. The people who supported and inspired you along the way. The lessons learned from challenges and setbacks. The growth and transformation you've experienced. Gratitude not only helps you celebrate yourachievements but also cultivates a positive outlook and a sense of contentment.

While celebrating your achievements is essential, it's equally important to set new goals that will continue to propel you forward on your journey. Before setting new goals, reflect on your core values and principles. Considerhow your values have guided you thus far and how they may shape your future goals. Align your new goals with your values to ensure they resonate with your true self. Take stock of your past achievements and the lessons learned along the way. Recognize the skills, knowledge, and experience you've gained. This self-assessment can inform your new goals and help you build on your strengths. Dreams are the fuel for setting new goals. Let your imagination run wild and envision what you want toachieve in various aspects of your life. Allow yourself to DREAM BIG and aim high, even if your goals initially seem ambitious. Not all goals are created equal. Prioritize your new goals based on their significance, alignment with your values, and feasibility. Consider which goals are most important to you at this stage of your journey.

SMART GOALS (Specific, Measurable, Achievable, Relevant, Time-bound) goals provide a clear framework for goal setting. Ensure that your new goals are specific, measurable, attainable, relevant to your aspirations, and have a defined timeline for completion. Large goals can beoverwhelming. Break them down into smaller, manageable steps or milestones. This approach makes it easier to track your progress and stay motivated. Inspiration can come from various sources, such as books, mentors, or role models. Draw inspiration from the writings of Daisaku Ikeda, who encourages continuous growth and the pursuit of noble aspirations. An action plan outlines the steps you need to take to achieve your goals. Specify the actions, resources, and timelines required for each goal. Having a plan in place increases your chances of success. Life is dynamic, and circumstances can change. Be open to adjusting your goals as needed to adapt to changing situations. Flexibility is a valuable trait in goal setting. Pursuing new goals may involve challenges and setbacks. Cultivate resilience by maintaining a positive mindset, learning from failures, and staying committed to your aspirations.

Celebrating your achievements and setting new goals is a cyclical process that propels you forward on your dream journey. Each cycle of achievement builds your confidence and self-belief. Reinforces your commitment to personal growth. Expands your horizons and possibilities. Fosters a sense of purpose and direction. Embrace this cycle with enthusiasm and a sense of adventure. Celebrate your achievements as milestones on your journey, and let them inspire you to set new, even more inspiring goals. In doing so, you continue to manifest abundance in every aspect of your life, realizing the full potential of the Dream Positioning System and the power within you.

Incorporating the practice of celebrating achievements and setting new goals into your DPS journey ensures that you remain on a path of growth, purpose, and fulfillment. It transforms your life into a continuous cycle of aspiration, action, and celebration, creating a fulfilling and meaningful existence.

"Every goal achieved is a steppingstone to the nextaspiration. Keep setting new goals, for they are thestars that guide you through life's journey."

- Daisaku Ikeda

THE END